LEVELS 2 AND 3

My ASL Book

A Communicative Approach for Learning a Visual Language

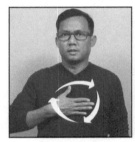

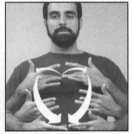

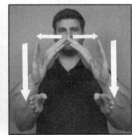

Don Bangs, PhD
Santa Rosa Junior College
Cabrillo College

With Contributions by

Donna Clendennin
Santa Rosa Junior College

Dolph Rehkop
Santa Rosa Junior College

Kendall Hunt
publishing company

Photographers/Videographers: Don Bangs
                                Jonih Renggono

Signing Models
Courtney Blaettler   Brenda Lyons
Therese Brown   Matthew MacDonald
Barbara Carpenter   Rey Montenegro
Donna Clendennin   Dolph Rehkop
Ismaeline Dianunu   Jonih Renggono
Joseph Dutson   Tuamana Ruhaka
Sherry Jo Hays   Noemi Sanchez
Antony Johnson   Sandra Thrapp
Karem Takhar Johnson   Madan Vasishta
James Kelly   Patrick Vital
Pui-Lam Lai   Barbara White
Justin Lee   Marlayne Williams

Image Credits:
Cover: Background cover image © Shutterstock.com, all other © Don Bangs
Interior: "Miss ASLey" © Mikhail Pogosov/Shutterstock.com, all signing images © Don Bangs,
clip art on pages 4, 6, 7, 8, 50, 54, 57 © Shutterstock.com, photos on page 166 © Shutterstock.com
Calendar image on page 9 and 188 © Milan M/Shutterstock.com

Kendall Hunt
publishing company

www.kendallhunt.com
Send all inquiries to:
4050 Westmark Drive
Dubuque, IA 52004-1840

Copyright © 2018 by Donald Bangs

PAK ISBN 978-1-5249-5115-3
Text ISBN 978-1-5249-5114-6

Published in the United States of America

CONTENTS

CHAPTER 5: LIVING IN THE "WORKING AND PLAYING BOXES" OF THE DEAF WORLD 181

CHAPTER 6: BECOMING AN ALLY TO THE DEAF WORLD 219

AUTHOR BIOGRAPHY

Don Bangs first began teaching ASL in 1965 when, as a junior at Gallaudet College (now University), he was drafted to teach a summer school ASL class. This year marks his fifty-second year of teaching ASL, Deaf culture, sign language translation, and a variety of other Deaf-related courses in colleges, universities, and theaters across the country. One of his goals in life is to make the world a more Deaf-friendly place. He is most grateful to all his students who showed him what worked or didn't work for helping Deaf and hearing people become life-long communicators in ASL. A proud 1966 Gallaudet graduate, he holds several advanced degrees, all with a Deaf focus, from University of Tennessee (MS, Deaf Education), University of Texas (MA, Radio-TV-Film), and University of California at Berkeley (PhD, Dramatic Art). He also holds a Professional Certificate for Teaching English as a Second/Foreign Language from: UC Berkeley. He has developed eighteen professionally produced plays and television programs in ASL and voice dealing with Deaf cultural issues and has translated over forty theater works and television programs from English to ASL and vice versa. He also served as a trainer, consultant, and developer for ASL and interpreter for education programs throughout the United States as well as in Brazil, Canada, Malaysia, Singapore, and Thailand.

Image © Don Bangs

CHAPTER 1

Celebrating Deaf People

INTRODUCTION TO THE CHAPTER

Perhaps you've read the expression "Life is a Celebration," an expression that has woven itself into American stories and songs for a long, long time. As early as 1855, Walt Whitman wrote "Song of Myself" in which his very first line was

"I celebrate myself and I sing myself"

Down through the century-and-a-half since, authors, actors, and songsters have used their works to encourage us to celebrate life. You may remember Rick Springfield's popular song, "Life is a Celebration" or the words of Maya Angelou, a Pulitzer-Prize-winning African-American writer and performer who wrote:

How important it is for us to recognize and celebrate our heroes and she-roes!

Or recall what Elaine Stritch, a beloved Broadway actress, thinks about celebrating:

I love holidays in New York. I love 'em. I want to celebrate something all the time, and New York has holidays for every day of the week, practically.

Or read Rishika Jain's "Inspirations" which explores the idea of life as a celebration. (See her poetry at rishikajain.com)

It all sounds like a great idea: just assume a positive attitude and celebrate the lives of everybody, and everything will be wonderful, hands down—or is it hands up and waving?

However, when hearing people talk about Deaf people, "Life is a Celebration" is not one of the first things that comes to their minds. In my ASL classes, when I teach the sign for "celebration" and I sign "Deaf life is a celebration," my hearing students react with bewilderment and exasperation. Some have challenged me, "How can you say Deaf life is a celebration when not being able to hear anything is such a sad thing. If I lost my hearing, I'd go crazy." Others have felt that the things to celebrate are new medical advances which can restore hearing. Or that we should celebrate people who were able to succeed "despite their hearing impairment."

It's not surprising that hearing students feel this way. They may have developed negative and limiting beliefs about Deaf people as a result of the influence of:

1. Negative portrayals of Deaf people in the media. This includes numerous books, newspaper articles, Facebook posts, movies, television shows, and other forms of media that definitely do not celebrate being Deaf. Here are some typical headlines and titles:

Heroic efforts to rescue Deaf people from the tragedy of deafness by various hearing family members and professionals

New technological inventions which restore the hearing of so many poor unfortunate Deaf people

Success stories about Deaf people who overcame their tragic handicap and succeeded in some challenging endeavor despite their deafness

Or many other examples of such ilk.

Even publications by some Deaf newspapers buy into this negative view of Deaf people. For example, if we peruse the items in a major online news service called "Deaf Weekly" in a one-month timeline, we'll find newspaper stories and articles with titles such as:

Deaf-Mute Capital Murder Suspect Incapable of Standing Trial

Deaf Boy Hears for the First Time and Skypes Guatemalan Family

Stroudsburg School Mom Says Walk to Bus Jeopardizes Deaf Son's Life

Altercation Between Two Deaf Men Leads to a Stabbing at a Birmingham Church

As still another example, we can read Carson McCuller's "The Heart is a Lonely Hunter," a required staple of many high school literature classes. This novel tells the story of a Deaf man, John Singer, who lives a lonely life in a small-town boarding house. He patiently listens to hearing townspeople who often came to his room to talk to him about their problems. None of these "friends" of John Singer can sign, but he "listens" to their stories, nodding sympathetically even though he does not understand a word they are saying. They feel free to tell him their deepest secrets, secure in the knowledge that Deaf John Singer will never reveal their confidences. John Singer does have one Deaf friend, an inmate in a mental hospital. However, when that friend dies, Singer, lonely and in despair, kills himself. Like many hearing authors, Carson McCullers can only conceive of Deaf people as tragic figures in sorrowful situations.

Clearly, mainstream literature and media are not ready to celebrate the lives of Deaf people in any meaningful way. Imagine how much better things would be if they did celebrate.

2. Negative experiences with Deaf people or negative stories from family and friends. Quite a few people think Deaf people are rude or ignorant. For example, when a hearing person calls out to a Deaf person who is not aware of it, the Deaf person probably will not respond, leading the hearing person to assume he/she does not have manners. Or hearing people may have struggled to communicate with Deaf people and will assume that they are stupid or retarded.

3. Wrong information from so-called medical, audiological and special educational "professionals." Their single-minded vision and goal is to restore deaf people to life as pseudo-hearing people, rather than simply accepting that Deaf people already live happy and satisfying lives as Deaf people. There are a multitude of stories about Deaf "oral failures" who discovered American Sign Language and Deaf people and went on to great success in their chosen fields.

So, instead of holding these negative beliefs about Deaf people, it is time to celebrate their lives.

Some of you may ask: What IS there to celebrate about being Deaf? That is the whole point of this first chapter. We are going to look at the idea of celebrations in our American culture and develop some communicative tools that will enable us to celebrate both hearing and Deaf people and their cultural worlds. After you finish this chapter, you will be able to use ASL to:

1. **Communicate information about various months and seasons.**

2. **Identify various holidays celebrated by both hearing and Deaf Americans and identify the month or months in which these holidays take place.**

3. **Describe various sports, hobbies, educational activities, places to go to, and other activities and destinations that Deaf people are involved in as a way to celebrate life or just to enjoy being with Deaf and hearing friends and families.**

4. **Communicate how you feel about various events and activities.**

5. **Use one of sixteen new adjectives to evaluate the quality of events and activities.**

6. **Identify and describe various Deaf holidays and celebrations on a local, regional, state-wide, and national level.**

7. **Use Non-Manual Markers as adverbs to describe how various actions were performed.**

8. **Describe the features of Deaf culture that demonstrate a "Deaf Gain" as opposed to a "Hearing Loss."**

9. **Outline some of the benefits that Deaf people and Deaf culture can offer to hearing people and society in general.**

10. **Identify or produce a variety of lexicalized finger-spelling signs and specify which parameter was changed to produce each sign.**

11. **Describe the meaning of various coordinating conjunctions and use them to combine different pairs of ASL sentences.**

12. **Outline the differences between "deafness" and "deafhood" perspectives.**

13. **Narrate a story about earthquakes and tornados and misunderstandings between a hearing mother and her Deaf son.**

14. **Narrate a brief history of the Deaf President Now movement and its impact on the power structure of the Deaf and hearing worlds.**

THE CLASSROOM

SEASONS AND MONTHS

To start on the pathway toward celebrating Deaf people, let's look at how the American people, both Deaf and hearing, celebrate holidays. As we shall see, there is a wide diversity of holidays as well as ways to celebrate these holidays. Before you can chat with Deaf friends about holiday celebrations, you need to learn the signs for the four seasons as well as for the months of the year.

Please view My ASL Tube 1-1 and learn the signs for these seasons:

My ASL Tube 1-1: SIGNS FOR SEASONS

Here are the signs you learned:

© Shutterstock

© Shutterstock

© Shutterstock

© Shutterstock

These signs are easy to remember because they are somewhat iconic. In other words, the signs suggest a visual image for each season. The sign for "winter" suggests cold weather, "Spring" suggests birth and growth of new plants; "Summer" suggests wiping one's brow from the heat; and "Fall" suggests leaves falling from a tree. Bear in mind that the vast majority of signs are not iconic. If they were, hearing people would easily be able to learn them!

In contrast to seasons, the signs for various months are not iconic at all. In fact, they are finger-spelled names and abbreviations. Here is a chart:

Month	Finger-Spelled Form	Month	Finger-Spelled Form
January	J-A-N	July	J-U-L-Y
February	F-E-B	August	A-U-G
March	M-A-R-C-H	September	S-E-P-T
April	A-P-R-I-L	October	O-C-T
May	M-A-Y	November	N-O-V
June	J-U-N-E	December	D-E-C

Let's play two games to practice your skills in communicating about months and seasons in ASL. Work with a partner. You and your partner can challenge each other to read and produce the signs for various months and seasons. In the first game, when your partner signs a specific month, you respond with the season that the month is a part of. Then the two of you switch roles. In the second game, your partner signs a specific season and you respond with the months in the season. Then the two of you switch roles. View My ASL Tube 1-2 to see how these questions and answers are signed:

My ASL Tube 1-2: DIALOGUES ABOUT MONTHS AND SEASONS

Here are some examples of the dialogues you saw in My ASL Tube:

Dialogue 1. Student A: *(Month) happens during <u>which season?</u>*
Student B: *(Month) happens during (Season)*

Example of Dialogue 1
Student A: *October happens during <u>which season?</u>*
Student B: *October happens during Fall.*

Dialogue 2. Student A: *(Season), <u>which months</u>?*
Student B: *(Season), months (1. _____; 2. _____; 3. _____)*

Example of Dialogue 2
Student A: *Summer, <u>which months</u>?*
Student B: *Summer months 1. June; 2. July; 3. August*

When doing the dialogue, don't forget these very important points:

1. When you ask a "Wh" question, be sure to use the "WH" NMM (Non-Manual Marker)

2. When you respond to the question in dialogue 2 by giving a list of months, be sure to show a "3" in your non-dominant hand and point to each finger as you spell the months. This is a listing technique similar to the one you used when you chatted about family members in *My ASL Book, Level 1*, Chapter 4.

Now, go ahead and practice with your partner.

CELEBRATING HOLIDAYS

Deaf people celebrate the same general holidays as hearing people do. However, they often adapt holiday celebrations to meet their needs as Deaf people. They may join hearing festivities or they may have their own celebrations, apart from those of hearing people. They need to feel welcome and to be assured that communication won't be a hassle. If your ASL skills are good and you are invited to join the Deaf celebration, grab the opportunity! You'll gain a valuable experience interacting with Deaf people. Of course, you'll need to know the signs for various holidays in order to celebrate with your Deaf friends. View My ASL Tube 1-3 to learn the signs for these holidays.

My ASL Tube 1-3: SIGNS FOR VARIOUS HOLIDAYS

Here are the holiday signs you learned, arranged by months:

JANUARY:

© Shutterstock

© Shutterstock

FEBRUARY:

 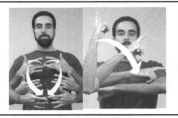

© Shutterstock

© Shutterstock

 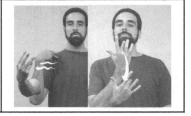

© Shutterstock

 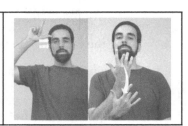

© Shutterstock

FEBRUARY OR MARCH:

 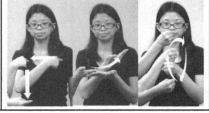

© Shutterstock

MARCH:

 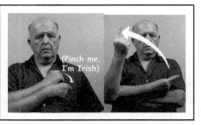

© Shutterstock

MARCH OR APRIL:

© Shutterstock

© Shutterstock

APRIL:

© Shutterstock

MAY:

© Shutterstock

MAY:

© Shutterstock

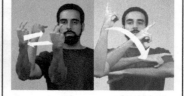

© Shutterstock

MAY/JUNE:

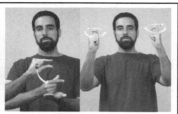

© Shutterstock

JUNE:

© Shutterstock

JULY:

© Shutterstock

SEPTEMBER:

© Shutterstock

SEPTEMBER/OCTOBER:

© Shutterstock

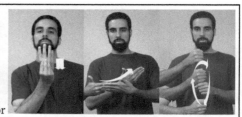

© Shutterstock

OCTOBER:

© Shutterstock

NOVEMBER:

 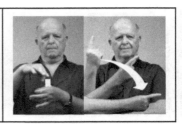

© Shutterstock

NOVEMBER:

Dia de los Muertos (fingerspell)

© Shutterstock

NOVEMBER:

© Shutterstock

NOVEMBER:

  or

© Shutterstock

NOVEMBER/DECEMBER:

(Flick open/closed eight)

© Shutterstock

NOVEMBER/DECEMBER:

© Shutterstock

DECEMBER:

© Shutterstock

DECEMBER:

© Shutterstock

DATE OF EVENT VARIES:

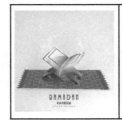  or

Ramadan (fingerspell)

© Shutterstock

Now, practice all the signs you learned with a partner, using the one-year blank calendar below. You and your partner can ask each other questions about holidays and when they take place during the year. View My ASL Tube 1-4 to see how questions and answers are signed:

My ASL Tube 1-4: DIALOGUES ABOUT MONTHS AND HOLIDAYS

Here are some examples of what you saw in My ASL Tube:

Dialogue 1:   Student A: *(Holiday) happens when?*
                    Student B: *(Holiday) happens (point to correct place on the calendar).*

Example of Dialogue 1
                    Student A: *Father's Day happens when?*
                    Student B: *Father's Day happens (point to June on the calendar).*

Dialogue 2:   Student A: *(Point to location on the calendar), holiday what?*
                    Student B: *(Point to location), holiday: 1. Holiday; 2. Holiday; 3. Holiday*

Example of Dialogue 2
                    Student A: *(Point to December), holiday what?*
                    Student B: *(Point to December), holiday: 1. Channukah; 2. Christmas; 3. Kwanzaa*

Here is the calendar:

This Year

JANUARY
Sun Mon Tue Wed Thu Fri Sat
1 2
3 4 5 6 7 8 9
10 11 12 13 14 15 16
17 18 19 20 21 22 23
24 25 26 27 28 29 30
31

FEBRUARY
Sun Mon Tue Wed Thu Fri Sat
1 2 3 4 5 6
7 8 9 10 11 12 13
14 15 16 17 18 19 20
21 22 23 24 25 26 27
28 29

MARCH
Sun Mon Tue Wed Thu Fri Sat
1 2 3 4 5
6 7 8 9 10 11 12
13 14 15 16 17 18 19
20 21 22 23 24 25 26
27 28 29 30 31

APRIL
Sun Mon Tue Wed Thu Fri Sat
1 2
3 4 5 6 7 8 9
10 11 12 13 14 15 16
17 18 19 20 21 22 23
24 25 26 27 28 29 30

MAY
Sun Mon Tue Wed Thu Fri Sat
1 2 3 4 5 6 7
8 9 10 11 12 13 14
15 16 17 18 19 20 21
22 23 24 25 26 27 28
29 30 31

JUNE
Sun Mon Tue Wed Thu Fri Sat
1 2 3 4
5 6 7 8 9 10 11
12 13 14 15 16 17 18
19 20 21 22 23 24 25
26 27 28 29 30

JULY
Sun Mon Tue Wed Thu Fri Sat
1 2
3 4 5 6 7 8 9
10 11 12 13 14 15 16
17 18 19 20 21 22 23
24 25 26 27 28 29 30
31

AUGUST
Sun Mon Tue Wed Thu Fri Sat
1 2 3 4 5 6
7 8 9 10 11 12 13
14 15 16 17 18 19 20
21 22 23 24 25 26 27
28 29 30 31

SEPTEMBER
Sun Mon Tue Wed Thu Fri Sat
1 2 3
4 5 6 7 8 9 10
11 12 13 14 15 16 17
18 19 20 21 22 23 24
25 26 27 28 29 30

OCTOBER
Sun Mon Tue Wed Thu Fri Sat
1
2 3 4 5 6 7 8
9 10 11 12 13 14 15
16 17 18 19 20 21 22
23 24 25 26 27 28 29
30 31

NOVEMBER
Sun Mon Tue Wed Thu Fri Sat
1 2 3 4 5
6 7 8 9 10 11 12
13 14 15 16 17 18 19
20 21 22 23 24 25 26
27 28 29 30

DECEMBER
Sun Mon Tue Wed Thu Fri Sat
1 2 3
4 5 6 7 8 9 10
11 12 13 14 15 16 17
18 19 20 21 22 23 24
25 26 27 28 29 30 31

Now you can communicate with your Deaf friends about various holidays. The next step is communicating what you do on these holidays. For some holidays, most people participate in traditional activities. For example, we celebrate Valentine's Day with cards and candy; Independence Day with parades, picnics, and pyrotechnics; and Thanksgiving with family and friends sitting down to festive dinners (and then sleeping off massive meals in front of the football games on TV).

A REVIEW OF EVENTS AND ACTIVITIES

But most holidays can be celebrated in a variety of ways. For this reason, we need to review all possible activities that people could participate in during a holiday or outside of a holiday. Here is a list from *My ASL Book, Level 1,* Chapter 5. Please review all the signs for these activities.

SPORTS AND RECREATION

GENERAL SPORTS: SPECTATOR OR PLAYER ACTIVITIES

Watch (two versions)	Play (a game)	Game

TEAM SPORTS

Baseball	Football	Basketball
Volleyball (two versions)	Soccer	Ice Hockey

SPORTS USING BOARDS, SKIS, OR SKATES

Skateboarding	Roller skating	Roller blading
Snowboarding	Downhill skiing	Cross-country skiing
Ice skating	Surfing	Water skiing

SPORTS USING PADDLES, RACKETS, CLUB, OR CUES

Ping-pong	Tennis	Golf
Pool		

COMBAT SPORTS

Fencing	Boxing	Karate
Wrestling		

OUTDOOR PHYSICAL RECREATION

Biking	Hiking	Running or jogging
Fishing	Hunting (two versions)	Mountain biking
Camping	Rock climbing	Horseback riding
Frisbee throwing	Bungee jumping	

WATER RECREATION

Diving	Swimming	Canoeing, kayaking
Sailing	Scuba diving	Snorkeling

MISCELLANEOUS

Aerobics	Archery	Bowling
Dancing	Exercising	Gymnastics
Hang gliding	Skydiving	Weight training

SOCIAL EVENTS AND ACTIVITIES

EVENTS

Formal party	Informal or lively party	Coffee gathering
Picnic (finger-spell)	Performance	Movie
Visiting (traveling to)	Visiting (chatting with)	Festival

VERBAL ACTIVITIES

Chatting casually	Chatting seriously	Playing cards
Playing games	Telling jokes	Telling stories

TAKING IN FOOD AND DRINK

Eating	Drinking wine or non-alcoholic beverages (verb form)
Drinking Beer (verb form)	Drinking liquor or cocktails (verb form)

PARTY BEVERAGES

Coffee	Tea	Milk
Cream	Sugar	Orange juice
Wine	Beer	Whiskey

SODA POP FLAVORS

Coke	Pepsi	Orange pop
Seven-Up	Sprite	Mountain Dew
Dr. Pepper	Root Beer	Ginger Ale

EDUCATIONAL ACTIVITIES AND EVENTS

Classes	Workshops	Lectures
In Connection with . . .		

HOBBIES

CREATIVE ARTS

Art	Drawing	Painting
Sculpture	Photography	Movie making
Performing	Singing	Magic

PRACTICAL ACTIVITIES

Cooking	Gardening	Making things
Sewing	Embroidery	Knitting

COLLECTING

Stamps	Rocks	Coins
Shells	Comics	

SPECTATOR ACTIVITIES

Reading	Watching TV	Playing computer games
Internet surfing	Listening to music	

RAISING AND TAKING CARE OF PETS

Cats	Dogs	Fish
Rabbits	Mice	Snakes

PLACES TO GO TO

Movie theater	Restaurant	Library
Department store	Bank	Mall
Laundromat	Post office	Church
Temple	Mosque	Park
Hospital	Doctor, nurse, or dentist's office	

Specialty stores: shoes, grocery, drugs, sports, computers, etc.

Let's practice identifying various holidays and some of the things that people do on these holidays. In My ASL Tube 1-5, three people are sitting around at a New Year's Eve party, sharing all the things they did during the past year. Watch the video and discover all the holidays that each of the three people celebrated and all the activities that they participated in during these holidays. Use this information to fill out the form below. You may find this video challenging, so it's a good idea to work in a small group to figure out what is being signed.

#. Holiday	Sharon's Activities	Wendy's Activities	Theresa's Activities
1.			
2.			
3.			
4.			
5.			
6.			
7.			
8.			
9.			
10.			
11.			
12.			
13.			
14.			
15.			
16.			
17.			
18.			

My ASL Tube 1-5: NEW YEAR'S EVE MEMORIES

How did you do? If you have become skilled at chatting about holidays and activities, you'll probably enjoy visiting with Deaf friends and acquaintances and sharing your experiences.

A REVIEW OF FEELINGS ABOUT EVENTS AND ACTIVITIES

There's one more thing you need to be able to communicate to your friends when you are chatting about holidays and activities: how you felt about the experience. Was it a fabulous experience or a frustrating one? Was it interesting or was it boring? Let's review the signs for how we feel about activities. View My ASL Tube 1-6 to review them.

MY ASL TUBE 1-6: A CONTINUUM OF FEELINGS AND INTEREST LEVELS

Here are the feeling level signs ranging from positive to neutral from MY ASL TUBE 1-6:

Here are the feeling signs ranging from neutral to negative from MY ASL TUBE 1-6:

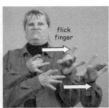

There is also a continuum of signs about interest levels, ranging from interesting to boring:

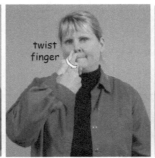

(The second sign means generally boring while the third sign means repetitively annoying.)

Take some time to review these signs. We'll play a game called "BFF Match." Here is how to play the game. The class breaks up into pairs and students in each pair try to create a profile of their partners by suggesting sports, social events, social activities, hobbies, and places to go to and asking if the partner enjoys these activities. Watch MAT 1-7 and see how you can ask your partners about how they felt about some activities:

MY ASL TUBE 1-7: CHATTING ABOUT ACTIVITIES

Here's what you saw in the video:

Example 1
> Student A: *Play volleyball, you enjoy?*
> Student B: *I hate it!*

Example 2
> Student A: *Gardening, you enjoy?*
> Student B: *It's just OK.*

Partners use the activity signs they recently reviewed and create a "dating profile," using the following form. If one partner likes an activity a lot, the other partner should circle the "+5"; if the partner dislikes an activity intensely, the other partner should circle the "–5"; if the partner feels somewhere between these two extremes, the other partner should circle the appropriate number:

ACTIVITY	LIKES OR DISLIKES (Circle one)										
Sports and Recreation	+5	+4	+3	+2	+1	0	–1	–2	–3	–4	–5
	+5	+4	+3	+2	+1	0	–1	–2	–3	–4	–5
	+5	+4	+3	+2	+1	0	–1	–2	–3	–4	–5
	+5	+4	+3	+2	+1	0	–1	–2	–3	–4	–5
	+5	+4	+3	+2	+1	0	–1	–2	–3	–4	–5
	+5	+4	+3	+2	+1	0	–1	–2	–3	–4	–5
Social Events/Activities	+5	+4	+3	+2	+1	0	–1	–2	–3	–4	–5
	+5	+4	+3	+2	+1	0	–1	–2	–3	–4	–5
	+5	+4	+3	+2	+1	0	–1	–2	–3	–4	–5
	+5	+4	+3	+2	+1	0	–1	–2	–3	–4	–5
	+5	+4	+3	+2	+1	0	–1	–2	–3	–4	–5
	+5	+4	+3	+2	+1	0	–1	–2	–3	–4	–5
Hobbies/Educational Activities	+5	+4	+3	+2	+1	0	–1	–2	–3	–4	–5
	+5	+4	+3	+2	+1	0	–1	–2	–3	–4	–5
	+5	+4	+3	+2	+1	0	–1	–2	–3	–4	–5
	+5	+4	+3	+2	+1	0	–1	–2	–3	–4	–5
	+5	+4	+3	+2	+1	0	–1	–2	–3	–4	–5
	+5	+4	+3	+2	+1	0	–1	–2	–3	–4	–5

Places to Go to	+5	+4	+3	+2	+1	0	−1	−2	−3	−4	−5
	+5	+4	+3	+2	+1	0	−1	−2	−3	−4	−5
	+5	+4	+3	+2	+1	0	−1	−2	−3	−4	−5
	+5	+4	+3	+2	+1	0	−1	−2	−3	−4	−5
	+5	+4	+3	+2	+1	0	−1	−2	−3	−4	−5
	+5	+4	+3	+2	+1	0	−1	−2	−3	−4	−5

After the partners have created each other's profile, they should share the results with the class. Other partners in the class should be on the alert and suggest their partners for a "BFF Match" if the profiles are similar. Eventually, all the people in class will be matched up with a new partner. Enjoy the game, but don't take it too seriously!!

EVALUATING THE QUALITY OF EVENTS AND ACTIVITIES

So far, we've reviewed all the signs about <u>how we feel</u> about an event activity. Let's learn some additional signs that help us to evaluate <u>the quality</u> of the event or activity itself. These evaluating signs range from the wonderful to the woebegone:

MY ASL TUBE 1-8: EVALUATING THE QUALITY OF ACTIVITIES OR EVENTS

Here are some of the signs you learned in My ASL Tube 1-8

POSITIVE EVALUATIONS

Fantastic   Thrilling   Fun   Want this again

Inspiring   Beautiful   Cool   Best

NEGATIVE EVALUATIONS

Lousy	Insignificant	Horrible	Never Again

Repulsive	Ugly	Creepy (eeek)	Worst

Now you have sixteen new signs that you can use when you chat with Deaf people about various events and activities and how good or bad they were. Let's watch a video of a Deaf couple as they share their ideas and thoughts about various events. Use the information from the video to fill out the chart.

What did A or B ask?	What was B or A's response/evaluation?
1.	
2.	
3.	
4.	
5.	
6.	
7.	
8.	
9.	
10.	
11.	
12.	
13.	
14.	
15.	
16.	

MY ASL TUBE 1-9: FRIENDS TALK ABOUT THE QUALITY OF ACTIVITIES AND EVENTS

Let's practice these new signs. Work with a partner. Partner A asks Partner B about which event or activity resulted in the most negative or positive evaluation. Then A and B switch roles. For this exercise, you can use the sign for "most" or "worst" with any of the qualities. We'll learn some other ways to express extreme evaluations later. Watch My ASL Tube and learn how to do the dialogue:

MY ASL TUBE 1-10: WHAT WAS THE MOST/WORST . . .?

Here is a sample of the conversations you saw in My ASL Tube 1-9

Example 1
    Student A: *You remember events since, most far-out event, what?*
    Student B: *Most far-out event what? I go-to Disneyland! (Describe the event)*

Example 2
    Student A: *You remember events since, most skin-crawling event, what?*
    Student B: *Most skin-crawling event, what? Halloween, 2011! (Describe the event)*

Example 3
    Student A: *You remember parties since, worst boring party, what?*
    Student B: *Worst boring party what? My Bible Class Party 2010! (Describe the event)*

Now, go ahead and interview your partner and use the information from your interview to fill out the following form:

#. Most/Worst	Event	When	Details
1. Fantastic			
2. Thrilling			
3. Fun			
4. Do-it-again			
5. Inspiring			
6. Beautiful			
7. Cool			
8. Best			
9. Lousy			
10. Insignificant			
11. Horrible			
12. Never again			
13. Repulsive			
14. Ugly			
15. Creepy			
16. Worst			

You and your partner can share each other's best and worst experiences with your classmates. Some of their stories will be predictable but other stories will be unexpected. You never know!

THE ASL CLUB

DEAF HOLIDAYS AND CELEBRATIONS

Deaf people who use ASL as their primary language comprise less than one percent of all Americans, but they organize and participate in an astonishing variety of events and activities. This is because they prize opportunities to get together and enjoy each other's company. There are Deaf organizations, programs, and activities for virtually every interest under the sun. Naturally, when Deaf people converse, a popular topic is the latest happenings and events at one of these clubs, programs, or organizations.

If you want to chat about these happenings or if you want to actually participate in any of them, you need to "brush up" on three important personal qualities that smooth the way. You learned about them in Chapter 4 of *My ASL Book, Level 1*. The qualities are:

1. Good ASL Skills

2. Awareness and understanding of Deaf people's experiences

3. Good attitudes

You will need these same qualities to participate in Deaf events and activities. Let's learn some signs that describe various Deaf special events and activities. Be sure to get plenty of rest before you start learning about them because, by the time you finish, you'll be exhausted (but happy). You've already reviewed the signs for a variety of social events earlier in the chapter. Here are some signs for additional popular Deaf events most of which involve sizeable numbers of Deaf and sign-skilled people. Watch My ASL Tube 1-11 to learn these signs.

MY ASL TUBE 1-11: POPULAR DEAF EVENTS

Here are the signs you learned ("Expo" is finger-spelled):

Conference   Deaf Awareness Day   Tournament   Banquet

Deaf School Homecoming   Open House   Fund-Raiser   Contest

Let's start out by describing some of the most important Deaf events that take place within the American Deaf Community:

CONFERENCES

Deaf people often get together in conferences to share information about their political, educational, religious, recreational, social, or what-have-you interests. Conferences can last anywhere from a few days to a week or more and can focus on local, regional, state-wide, national, or international interests. They tend to begin with an open plenary meeting featuring a well-respected speaker and end with some sort of luncheon or banquet. At one time, the get-togethers were called conventions, but many convention-goers could not get funding to support their participation, due to the more "social" nature of a convention. So most of these events are now called a more fundable "conference" even though they provide the fun and comradery of a convention. Here is just a partial list of Deaf organizations that conduct conferences along with how often they take place, the usual season that the conferences happen, and key websites:

National Association of the Deaf (Biannually during Summer of Even-numbered Years)

http://www.nad.org

The NAD calls itself "the nation's premier civil rights organization of, by and for deaf and hard of hearing individuals." It is actively involved with many issues of interest to Deaf and hard of hearing people. A NAD conference is designed to provide information about the latest advances in the Deaf world and conference events include plenary sessions, workshops, exhibitions, entertainment, and many other activities.

State Associations of the Deaf (Biannually during Odd-numbered Years)

Almost every state has a state association of the Deaf. You can learn a lot about the political and cultural issues of state and local Deaf communities from these associations. They work to resolve issues facing Deaf people and lobby for improved civil rights, accommodations, communications, and other services for Deaf citizens in their states. Most state associations have websites and you can use Google to find them.

Deaf School Alumni Associations (dates of Reunions Vary)

The alumni of many schools for Deaf children have formed a strong bond with their classmates and with other students at their school. Because of this, most schools have a fairly strong alumni association which supports a variety of activities including reunions, support for athletic activities, scholarship programs, and other support services. Some alumni associations have a strong influence on the development and success of Deaf school programs.

Deaf Seniors of America (Biannually During Odd-numbered Years)

http://www.deafseniorsofamerica.org

DSA works to improve the quality of life for Deaf senior citizens through seminars that deal with Deaf seniors' well-being and safety, awareness projects for decision makers, provision of service to the general public, and information sharing among Deaf seniors about resources that will contribute to their positive image and fuller participation in the mainstream society.

Ethnic and minority groups (Varies with Each Group)

Deaf people who are also members of some other minority groups are sometimes called "Deaf Plus." These people often have to juggle two identities: a Deaf cultural identity and a social or cultural identity of minority groups such as Latinos, African-American, LGBT people, and others. This can be a problem for Deaf members of some stigmatized minorities. For example, a Deaf gay man may have to deal with homophobia in a Deaf organization and keep his sexuality hidden. On the other hand, this Deaf gay man will face discrimination by hearing gay organizations, especially with respect to communication accessibility. He might want to participate in activities sponsored by this organization, only to be told that they don't have any funds available to pay for interpreters. So the Deaf gay man can encounter negative attitudes and behaviors in both his Deaf and gay worlds. Deaf members of other minority groups will experience these troubling situations to a greater or lesser extent.

There are so many Deaf minority organizations that I can only list some of the many websites available for further exploration. Also, you can review the signs for each minority group from *My ASL Book, Level 1,* Chapter 7:

> **Women:** Deaf Women United; http://www.dwu.org
>
> **Gay and Lesbian People:** Rainbow Alliance of the Deaf; http://www.deafrad.org
>
> **Lesbians:** Deaf Lesbian Festival; http://www.deaflesbianfestival.org
>
> **Bisexual, Transgendered, Transsexual:** Deaf Queer Resource Center; http://www.deafqueer.org
>
> **African American:** National Black Deaf Advocates; http://www.nbda.org
>
> **Asian American:** National Asian Deaf Congress; http://www.nadcusa.org
>
> **Hispanic American:** http://www.deafvision.net/aztlan/resources
>
> **Native American:** Sacred Circle: http://www.deafnative.com/mission.html
>
> **Deaf-blind people:** American Association of the Deaf-Blind: http://www.aadb.org

Religious Groups and Conferences (Varies with Each Group)

Deaf church-goers often have a complicated relationship with their churches, temples, mosques, and other religious organizations. On the one hand, these religious organizations may be able to meet the spiritual needs of their Deaf members as well as sponsor various ceremonies such as services, baptisms, marriages, funerals, memorial services, and other ceremonies. On the other hand, some religious organizations treat their Deaf members as second-class citizens who need the blessings of the church or temple or mosque to be saved from their pitiful conditions.

The most popular religious groups have leaders who are themselves Deaf or who are fluent in sign language and knowledgeable and sensitive to the culture of Deaf people. These religious organizations can tailor their weekly services and special ceremonies to meet the communication needs of their Deaf members. Additionally, they provide a social support network. Generally, the services and ceremonies are conducted in ASL and arranged to maximize visual information-sharing among the members. Surprisingly, some religious organizations sponsor choirs that "sing" various hymns and songs in sign language, often accompanied by a drum for keeping pace.

Many of these Deaf and Deaf-aware leaders work together to create national and international fellowship among all Deaf practitioners of their faith. And conferences serve as places to share spiritual ideas and feelings with one another. To help you interact with people of your chosen faith, watch My ASL Tube 1-12 and learn all the signs for the various religions.

MY ASL TUBE 1-12: VARIOUS RELIGIOUS DENOMINATIONS

Here are all the religious denominations you learned about in My ASL Tube

For other religions, Deaf people finger-spell the abbreviations. For example: Seventh Day Adventists = SDA.

Below is only a partial list of all the religious organizations serving Deaf people which also have conferences from time to time.

Catholic: International Deaf Catholic Association—US: http://www.icda-us.org

Southern Baptist: Southern Baptist Conference of the Deaf: http://www.sbcdeaf.org

Methodist: United Methodist Congress of the Deaf: http://www.umcd.org

Lutheran: International Deaf Lutherans Association: http://deafjesus.org/ilda/ILDAhome.html

Episcopal: Episcopal Conference of the Deaf: http://www.ecdeaf.org

Church of Latter Day Saints: DLDS: http://www.deaflds.org/

Seventh Day Adventist: Three Angels Deaf Ministries: http://www.deafadventist.org/

Jews: Jewish Deaf Congress: http://jewishdeafcongress.org

Muslims: Global Deaf Muslims: http://www.globaldeafmuslim.org

EXPOS

Over the past fifteen years, Deaf and ASL expos have become popular ways to disseminate new ideas and new technology to various Deaf communities. They have also become effective meeting places for Deaf people to reunite with one another, catch up on news, and enjoy performances and presentations by popular entertainers. They are excellent places for ASL students to improve their skills and learn more about Deaf culture in a low-stress environment.

A Deaf or ASL expo generally draws anywhere from 1,000–10,000 people—Deaf, hearing, sign-language students, parents of deaf children, and other people from all walks of life. You'll find a variety of booths featuring the latest communication technology; local and national Deaf political, religious, and service organizations; sellers of Deaf books, videos, and DVDs; entertainment programs; and many more things to see and opportunities to participate. It can be an overwhelming and intimidating experience for new ASL students, but, if you are patient and stay open to new challenges, you'll learn a lot. Here are companies that organize expos.

DeafNation expo: http://deafnation.com

Probably the granddaddy of Deaf expos, this media organization was founded by two Deaf brothers, Joel and Jed Barish, and sponsored annual tours of ten to fifteen expos to major cities and regions all over the United States. Admission to the expo was free of charge. These expos provided Deaf people with wonderful opportunities to learn about new products and services, meet old friends and classmates, watch and participate in live shows by well-known performing artists, and maintain their network of Deaf world connections. In 2015, DeafNation formed a partnership with a business called Language People, but relations quickly turned bitter and DeafNation ended up suing Language People. As a result, the expos have been suspended.

DeafNation also produces a video program called "No Barriers" where Joel travels to various locations around the world and interviews Deaf people about their communities and cultures.

TERPexpo: http://www.terpexpo.com

This group manages events and conferences that focus on professional training for sign language interpreters. Their expos take place in a wide variety of locations across the country and offer a wide selection of workshops and presentations on interpreting.

State-wide, regional, and local expos

A substantial number of organizations sponsor these expos. They are too numerous to mention. You can find them by googling "state/region/city + Deaf expos"

TOURNAMENTS

For virtually every popular sport, Deaf people will organize a tournament, either among themselves, or competing against hearing sports groups. Currently, Deaf organizations support local, regional, and national tournaments in sports such as basketball, softball, volleyball, and soccer. The International Committee of Sports for the Deaf sponsors both summer and winter international Deaf games called Deaflympics. In the most recent winter Olympics in Salt Lake City, Utah, in 2007, 298 athletes from 23 countries competed in 27 events. The summer Olympics in Taipei, Taiwan, in 2009 was even more impressive; 2,493 athletes from 77 countries competed in 177 events. Another organization, the World Recreational Association of the Deaf recently celebrated a twenty-five-year history of recreational activities with a huge masquerade ball in Las Vegas. You can find more information about tournaments and other sports competitions by googling "Deaf," "sports," "recreation," "deaflympics," "tournament," etc.

DEAF AWARENESS DAY/WEEK/MONTH

The World Federation of the Deaf (WFD) sponsored its first International Day of the Deaf in 1958 and later expanded this to an International Week of the Deaf. Deaf and hearing people around the world observe this celebration during the last full week of September and mark the International Day of the Deaf on the last Sunday of the week. American organizations have renamed this as Deaf Awareness Day, Week, or Month.

According to WFD, the purpose of International Week of the Deaf is to promote the achievements of Deaf people and the concerns of the Deaf community to government and educational leaders as well as the general public. During this week, Deaf organizations carry out information campaigns about their work, and publicize Deaf concerns and issues. This special week also helps to increase cooperation and support among Deaf people and their hearing allies and to promote the rights of Deaf people throughout the world.

OTHER LOCAL AND REGIONAL DEAF CELEBRATIONS

Luncheons and Banquets: These are popular annual affairs, especially with senior citizens and special interest groups. There may or may not be a Deaf speaker.

Deaf School Celebrations: Homecomings and Reunions: Most residential schools for Deaf children reserve one football game in the fall as the homecoming game, usually against a rival school. Also, from time to time, Deaf school alumni come together in a reunion and have a wonderful time sharing school stories and catching up on Deaf news.

Open Houses: These are hosted by various schools, organizations, and agencies and often happen during Deaf Awareness Week or as part of Christmas festivities.

Fund-raisers and contests: Many Deaf organizations must survive through a variety of events and activities that raise funds for various expenses. There is no limit to the scope and variety of activities that can benefit these organizations.

On the next My ASL Tube, two people will be chatting at a New Year's Eve party and looking back on all that happened over the past year. Watch the video and fill out the following form.

Person A's Event	Level of Enjoyment	Person B's Event	Level of Enjoyment
1.			
2.			
3.			
4.			
5.			
6.			
7.			
8.			
9.			
10.			

MY ASL TUBE 1-13 LAST YEAR'S EVENTS AND HOW MUCH I ENJOYED THEM

Now it's your turn to chat about events, activities, and how well you enjoyed them. Work with a partner and share your own year-end review of Deaf and hearing events. Write down ten real or imaginary events, activities, and evaluations from your past year. You and your partner can share each other's events, activities, and evaluations with each other. As an optional activity, each student can chat with other students about his/her partner's year-end review. If each partner is creative, the sharing can be fun and funny!

Event	YOU		Event	YOUR PARTNER	
	Activity	Evaluation		Activity	Evaluation
1.					
2.					
3.					
4.					
5.					
6.					
7.					
8.					
9.					
10.					

ASL IN YOUR FACE

USING NMMS AS ADVERBS

What a lot of events and activities to chat about with your Deaf friends!! Of course, not all events and activities are exciting or enjoyable or fun. Sometimes they can be boring or frightening or unpleasant. Naturally you may want to express how you participate in an activity. For that, you may need NMM adverbs. For example, you might have chatted as you ***normally*** do, or you might be stuck with chores and do them ***carelessly***, or, while skiing, you might have missed the black diamond sign and be forced to ski ***fearfully*** down an almost vertical trail. Your friends use adverbs to add color to their stories about past events and activities and you can do this, too.

Amazingly, you can use NMMs as adverbs to show how you performed an activity. There are many, many NMM adverbs, but we'll show six of them this time. You will learn other adverbs as you observe Deaf people narrating stories or happenings. Watch My ASL Tube to learn about these adverbs. In this video, a Deaf man will describe a cross-country skiing trip from the top of a mountain to the base. He'll use NMMs to show how he skied.

My ASL Tube 1-14: SIX NMM ADVERBS

Here are the six NMMs you saw in the video of the skier:

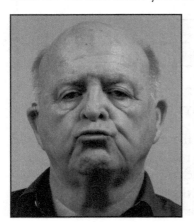

adverb: normally, regularly, confidently

adverb: freely, pleasurably enthusiastically

adverb: strenuously, struggling against a tough obstacle

adverb: carefully, with concentration

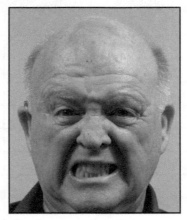

adverb: struggling apprehensively

adverb: carelessly, recklessly

Did you grasp how these NMMs function like adverbs for the skiing story? Practice each until it comes to you automatically. Think of situations where you did something normally, freely, strenuously, carefully, apprehensively, or carelessly and tell a Deaf friend what you did, adding the appropriate NMM adverbs. Your friend will ask with amazement, "Where did you learn that?"

Now, let's apply what we learned about NMM adverbs. We'll watch My ASL Tube and view Deaf people talking about their experiences, using NMM adverbs. Below is a table with two columns. The first column is for an event or activity and the second is for an adverb that describes how an activity was performed. Watch My ASL Tube and use the information to fill in the form.

#. Event or Activity	How the signer acted (NMM adverb)
1.	
2.	
3.	
4.	
5.	
6.	
7.	
8.	
9.	
10.	
11.	
12.	

My ASL Tube 1-15: EVENTS, ACTIVITIES, AND NMM ADVERBS

How well did you do with this exercise? If you had problems, go back and view the story again. Or work with your instructor or another ASL student to clarify various NMM adverbs

Here is a fun exercise for you to integrate NMM adverbs, events, and activities into an anecdote or story. Work with a partner. Think of some special event or day, such as Independence Day, Halloween, Spring Break, etc. Tell your partner what activities you participated in during that special event. With each activity, add on an NMM adverb. You might need to explain why you used a certain NMM adverb. For example, "My friends invited me to go swimming in the ocean. I swam+enjoyment NMM adverb." But I saw a shark! "So, I swam+NMM 'ee' adverb" to show that you swam as fast as you could to shore). You can make the story entertaining and fun for your partner.

DEAF MYTHBUSTERS

The Deaf community has been buzzing about a new idea: "Deaf Gain." Instead of saying that a person has a "hearing loss," Deaf people are saying the person has a "Deaf gain." What gives? How can losing one's hearing be considered a gain?

"Deaf Gain" is a concept developed by scholars at Gallaudet University led by H. Dirksen Bauman and Joseph Murray. It proposes an alternative framework for perceiving Deaf people and their right to exist in our modern world. This movement seeks to replace the negative framework of "hearing loss" with a positive framework, "Deaf gain."

Throughout history, medical and educational "experts" have made it their goal to transform Deaf people into copies of "normal" hearing people. Because of their belief that Deaf people suffer from a deficiency which impairs their ability to function as normal people, they have made every effort to repair the "damage" and restore the speech and hearing of every Deaf individual. Ironically, this attitude has led to programs and policies that have often damaged Deaf people by depriving them of their own language and culture. Their many well-meaning crimes of compassion include banning sign languages; forcing unwilling Deaf students to rely on unreliable auditory devices in order to communicate exclusively through speech and hearing; subjecting Deaf children to unwanted auditory surgery; isolating Deaf children from their Deaf peers in order to prevent them from learning signs; and many other misguided activities.

Deaf people are not the only victims of the "normalcy" game. Many other minority groups have also suffered. For example, during one period of their history, Native American children were taken from their families and forced to attend boarding schools where white educators made every effort to expunge the "Indian-ness" of their language and culture. As another example, even today, in some schools, students from Spanish-speaking families are banned from speaking their native language out of the mistaken fear that speaking it will impair their learning of English.

The invasive belief in "normalcy" now threatens to eradicate Deaf people altogether. Over 100 deafness genes have been discovered and, frequently, embryos with these deaf genes are aborted. Additionally, if there is evidence of deafness in a family tree, genetic counseling services have discouraged parents from having children since they may give birth to a deaf baby. Even if a baby is unexpectedly born deaf, the parents are encouraged to "fix" the deafness. In some countries, entire populations of deaf babies are being implanted with cochlear devices and shunted off to hearing schools where they are not allowed to use sign language. To be very clear, a cochlear implant DOES NOT TRANSFORM DEAF PEOPLE INTO HEARING PEOPLE. A normal cochlea has over 10,000 hair cells which translate sound waves to nerve impulses. A cochlear implant has, at most, 22 nodes, so, for example, a Beethoven symphony will be transformed by a cochlear implant into a series of squeaks and whistles and Deaf people have to learn how to interpret these noises. By the way, Beethoven was deaf but I doubt he would have opted for a cochlear implant, if one was available.

All because the "experts" believe that "normalcy" is always the best choice for Deaf people. But is it? Would our society be a better place if it were completely devoid of sign language, Deaf people, and Deaf culture? I believe that the loss of this rich language and culture would be a tragedy. To understand this, let's turn to the concept of "Deaf Gain."

"Deaf Gain" simply means that Deaf people gain something by being Deaf. And hearing people also gain something by having Deaf people in their midst. And society as a whole gains something from having access to ASL and Deaf culture. What kind of gains? Let's look at just a rudimentary list. You'll find many more items as you continue your adventure in the Deaf world.

EFFECTIVE COMMUNICATION ABILITIES

Quite a few years ago, I obtained a position in a Disability Resources Department as a specialist providing support and accommodations to Deaf college students. Every month I was required to attend a department meeting and, since everyone else in the department was hearing and I was the only Deaf person, the department provided a sign language interpreter to facilitate communication between myself and the other department members.

So, I went to my first meeting—and what a meeting! It was total chaos because of a lot of dysfunctional communication habits. People were interrupting each other; two or more people were speaking at the same time; some people were having side conversations while the meeting was going on; and many other dysfunctional activities. My interpreter was going crazy trying to relay to me all this communication madness. Once I had recovered from the experience, I worked with the interpreter to try to resolve the communication problems created at the meeting. At the next meeting, the interpreter and I bluntly told the department that it was impossible for us to participate in the meeting because of the communication chaos. We requested that the meeting participants follow some basic ground rules which included: 1. Only one person was to speak at a time; 2. Participants had to raise their hands and be recognized before they could speak; and 3. Side conversations at the meeting were not allowed. Once the disabilities resources department followed these basic ground rules, the meeting went very smoothly.

After the meeting, several people approached me and thanked me for speaking out as they, too, had been having problems with the communication chaos of the meeting. So, by following Deaf rules for meetings, the Disability Resources Department received a "Deaf Gain."

I thought this was just a one-time situation. Imagine my surprise when, several years later, Dr. Bruno Kahne, an international business consultant and coach, came out with a book titled: ***Deaf Tips: Twelve lessons from the Deaf world to improve your communication in your personal, social, and professional life***. In his trail-blazing book, Dr. Kahne described an experiment where one group of three Deaf people and another group of three hearing people were each given six pictures and asked to work together to put the pictures in the correct order. The results were amazing: The Deaf group finished the task in less than two minutes, while the hearing group took over six minutes to complete the same task. Dr. Kahne repeated this experiment again and again with over 1,000 subjects and got the same results. Deaf groups took one-third the amount of time to complete the task than hearing people did.

Said Dr. Kahn, "Learning how to communicate more like a deaf person could improve your listening skills and make yourself heard better at work."

In an age where special education programs refer to Deaf people as people with communication disorders, how is it possible that Deaf people actually communicate among themselves more effectively than hearing people do? Could the "communication disorders" actually belong to the hearing people who frequently face problems in communicating with each other and with Deaf people? If hearing people could improve their communication abilities, imagine the impact on prospects for peace and good relations in the world!

Dr. Kahne identified twelve aspects of Deaf people's communication styles that made them better communicators. Due to space limitations, I will only describe a few and encourage you to buy his book. According to Dr. Kahne, Deaf people are more effective communicators because they are good at preparing physical and psychological spaces to facilitate communication; reading body language; being simple and precise; asking questions; focusing on the important issues; saying what they think; and many other communicative skills. If hearing Americans adopted many of the communicative skills of their Deaf counterparts, as Dr. Kahne suggests, we'd all be far better communicators!

SHARING AND CARING

Have you visited a Starbucks outlet lately? Or ridden on a bus or a subway train? Did you notice how human interactions such as sharing and caring have declined considerably over the past decade, thanks to smart phones and laptops? Tom Holcomb and Anna Mindess have developed a fascinating video titled "See What I Mean: Differences Between Deaf and Hearing Cultures." This video features many vignettes that show how cultural differences can cause conflicts between Deaf and hearing people. In several vignettes, we discover how hearing people who value their privacy clash with Deaf people who value information sharing. In one vignette, a Deaf man asks his hearing neighbor how much his new car cost only to be rebuffed by the neighbor who feels it is none of the Deaf man's business. In another vignette, a Deaf college professor comments that her hearing student looks rather ill and asks if she is okay, only to get the brush-off from the student who feels the Deaf professor should not pry into her personal life.

Most hearing Americans value independence and privacy, but, taken to extremes, this leads to isolation and loneliness. Deaf people value information sharing which shows that they care about the people they meet. If hearing people adopted some of these Deaf information-sharing and caring habits, their world might be a warmer and more welcoming place.

Information sharing and caring is not necessarily limited to spoken or signed information and can include physical actions. For example, two Deaf people who are chatting while walking down a sidewalk will take actions that two hearing people would not think about performing. The hearing friends will walk along while chatting away and looking straight ahead to watch out for obstacles that might trip them up. In contrast, Deaf people have to look at each other to be able to communicate. So, if the left partner is approaching an obstacle, the right partner will see it first, catch an arm and pull the left partner aside so he/she won't trip over the obstacle and vice versa. Imagine the warm feeling that each partner gets when his/partner shows how much he/she cares by protecting him from injury. It makes the world a warmer place full of caring people.

As another example, suppose you arrive late to a party where a group of people are gathered in a circle excitedly discussing or gossiping about some major development. Since you've arrived after a significant part of the discussion has taken place, you have no idea what is going on. What to do?

In the Deaf world, there's nothing to worry about. Almost always, the group will stop for a moment while one of the members gives you a brief summary of what has happened. Obviously the group cares about you and shares needed information so you'll feel a part of the group. This happens often, probably much more so than with hearing people. Again, you get a sense of warmth and belonging.

This is not to say that the Deaf world is Heaven on Earth. There can be rude Deaf people and unpleasant Deaf cultural experiences as in any culture. But it seems that the increased information sharing and caring helps create a better connection between people in the Deaf community.

EXPANDING THE RICHNESS OF COMMUNICATION AND LANGUAGE

Deaf people add to our cultural repertoire in many ways. For one thing, they offer a unique visual and gestural way of interacting with people. They also provide a fascinating cultural perspective. When hearing people are exposed to Deaf people, especially in sign language classes, their ideas about language and communication expand considerably. They become more adept at using gestures and in grasping visual skills. If they are lucky, they can appreciate ASL poetry and storytelling and even develop visual forms of literature themselves.

In sum, we should not be surprised when Deaf people resist the efforts of social and medical professionals to help them become pseudo-hearing people. In fact, we should support a diverse society which includes the rich culture of Deaf people. Our success as a society might very well depend on Deaf people just being who they are.

FINGER-SPELLING FINESSE

LEXICALIZED FINGER-SPELLING SIGNS

Deaf people sometimes adapt finger-spelled words and convert them into signs with their own unique characteristics. These are called "lexicalized finger-spelling signs." There are several ways to create a lexicalized sign. Basically, you use one of the sign language parameters to change a finger-spelled word into a lexicalized sign.

Do you remember from *My ASL Book, Level 1* that there are five parameters for each sign and changing a parameter will change the meaning of the sign. The parameters are: 1. Handshape; 2. Location; 3. Movement; 4. Orientation; and 5. Non-Manual Markers. Deaf people can use one or more of the first four parameters to transform finger-spelled words into lexicalized signs. Watch My ASL TUBE 1-16 and learn how this is done.

My ASL Tube 1-16: EXAMPLES OF LEXICALIZED FINGER-SPELLING SIGNS

Let's talk about the signs you saw in My ASL Tube 1-16.

HANDSHAPES: OMITTING OR BLENDING ONE OR MORE LETTERS.

If some finger-spelled words are used often, they are transformed into signs by omitting some letters, usually the middle letter or letters. Here are some examples. We will use "#" to indicate a finger-spelled word:

yes → #Y-S	but → #B-T	bank → #B-N-K	cool → #C-O-L
hurt → #H-T	sure → #S-R-E	what → #W-H-T	when → #W-H-N

This is not a complete list because many more lexicalized signs are being created over time. It's important to recognize that your Deaf friends may not always finger-spell words exactly as they are written but will modify them for quicker and more efficient communication. You might want to discuss with your ASL classmates some other loan signs that they have observed.

LOCATION: SHOWING A RELATIONSHIP BETWEEN FINGER-SPELLED WORDS AND SITUATIONS

Some relationships between words and situations are pretty obvious. For example, if a person is very hungry, we might finger-spell #F-O-O-D across the forehead to indicate that he/she is obsessed with food. Or, if someone is obsessed with sex, we will finger spell #s-e-x across the forehead. Some other examples of this type include #G-I-R-L-S, #B-O-Y-S and other examples.

ORIENTATION: BLENDING DIFFERENT POSITIONS

Certain letters such as "J" and "G" change their orientation when finger-spelled which can result in lexicalized signs. Additionally, the effort of changing an orientation can sometimes result in the loss of some finger-spelled letters. Here are some examples of orientation changes:

"G" words: dog → #D-G   gas → #G-S   leg → #L-G

"J" words: job → #J-B   jog → #J-G   junior → #J-R

MOVEMENT: CREATING MULTIPLE MEANINGS

This is probably the most creative area of loan signs. A good example is the word "back," finger-spelled as #B-A-K. This loan sign can be used in many contexts: "I'll be back" (finger-spelled inward toward the room); "He and she are back together" (both hands finger-spell the loan sign while coming together as in the sign for "meet"; or "Want your money back?" (finger-spelled from signer to receiver). Similarly, you can create the loan sign "no" → #N-O to show a specific person being denied permission or "knock out" → #K-O" to show a specific person hitting the dust or falling into bed.

In the next M.A.T. Video, you'll see people telling you about some event or activity. For each event or activity, the person telling the story will use a lexicalized sign. For each story, identify the sign, write down the meaning, and paraphrase the story or event in which the lexicalized sign appeared.

#. Lexicalized Sign	Meaning	The person's story or event
1.		
2.		
3.		
4.		
5.		
6.		
7.		
8.		
9.		
10.		
11.		
12.		
13.		
14.		
15.		

My ASL Tube 1-17: SOME ASL SENTENCES USING LEXICALIZED SIGNS

LINGUISTIC ILLUMINATIONS

ENGLISH LANGUAGE COORDINATING CONJUNCTIONS

Like English, ASL can combine two or more sentences into a new and more complex sentence using conjunctions. In this chapter, we'll focus on **Coordinating Conjunctions**. These are words that join two independent sentences or clauses to create a new sentence. The most common English conjunctions are "and," "but," "or," "so," and "yet." Deaf people have transformed these conjunctions by using unique signs or physical movement or both. Depending on your Deaf friends' language background, they may use a more "English-like" way to express a conjunction or they may express the conjunction in a more natural ASL form. Let's watch My ASL Tube 1-18 and see how this is done. We'll show you some variations of the most common conjunctions.

My ASL Tube 1-18: COMMON ENGLISH COORDINATING CONJUNCTIONS EXPRESSED IN ASL

Here are the variations of conjunctions that you saw in the video:

AND

"and" is English-like   "and" describes next item in a sequence   body shift: general purpose "and"   "and," what's more . . .

BUT

"but" as lexicalized sign   "but" as difference   "but" as a warning   "but" via body language

OR

Finger-spelled "or"

"or" as a list of choices

body shift: general "or"

SO

"so" finger-spelled

body shift: general "so"

ASL CONJUNCTIONS

ASL offers a number of conjunctions that do more than just link sentences; they also suggest intriguing and fascinating relationships between the two sentences that they are conjoining. Deaf people want to go beyond the bland "and" or "or" of English to create some fascinating transitions. Watch My ASL Tube 1-19 to learn about these conjunctions.

My ASL Tube 1–19: COMMON ASL CONJUNCTIONS

Here are the various common ASL conjunctions that you saw in the video:

Something negative happened

Plans were disrupted by a negative event

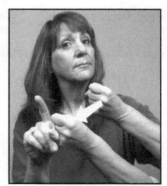
Something positive or neutral happened unexpectedly

A new event took
place or happened

Task or event completed
New task or event begins

An explanation for a
situation is found

While facing a situation,
a new thought appears

A new event or situation
takes the signer by surprise

While facing a situation
the signer is frustrated

Let's practice using these conjunctions. Watch My ASL Tube 1-19. In the video, a person will sign a sentence followed by a conjunction. Then the person will sign one of three possible second sentences. You need to determine which sentence "fits" with the first sentence and the conjunction. Use the information to fill out the form:

#. Conjunction	Meaning	Which sentence is next? (A, B, or C)
1.		
2.		
3.		
4.		
5.		
6.		
7.		
8.		
9.		
10.		
11.		
12.		

My ASL Tube 1-20: TELL US ABOUT THE CONJUNCTION

Now that you've learned fourteen signed conjunctions, you and small groups of your classmates can play a game called, "Add to the Story." Here is how it works: Student A narrates an event or situation and adds a conjunction. Student B has to create a new situation based on the previous sentence and conjunction. Student B adds a new conjunction after which Student C creates the appropriate situation, and so on. No conjunction can be repeated. The game continues until the group runs out of conjunctions. Then, a new game begins. Here is an example of this game:

> Student A: Yesterday, I rode my bike, **wrong-twist ...**

> Student B: The police stopped me and told me not to ride on the sidewalk, **but ...**

> Student C: I escaped and peddled away fast, **so ...**

And so on. Try it! It's fun!

ASK MISS ASLEY: THE DEAFINITE ANSWER

(Miss ASLey is a Deaf professional etiquettarian. She feels it is her duty to correct uninformed people whenever they make a faux pas about the culture of Deaf people and to show them the proper cultural behavior to exhibit toward the Deaf world. If you want to learn a properly balanced attitude toward Deaf people, Miss ASLey is who you need to consult with.)

Dear Miss ASLey,

I am a second-semester ASL student who loves to learn new things about ASL and Deaf culture. I decided to use Google to find out more information about Deaf people. So, I typed in "deafness" and looked through the results. But, I found mostly medical postings about the causes of hearing losses and how to cure hearing-impaired people. I told my Deaf friend Janet about my Google searches because I thought she would be pleased with my interest in Deaf people. But, she got upset. "Don't ever use that ugly word, 'deafness'!" she said. "Haven't you ever heard of 'deafhood'?" Then she walked off. I was stunned. What's wrong with the word "deafness"? People use it all the time.

Later I tried to meet her and ask her to explain what she meant but she was cold to me and refused to tell me. How can I get back into Janet's good graces? What the heck is Deafhood anyway?

Still Stunned Shunned Signing Student

Dear Still Stunned Shunned Signing Student (SSSSS),

Miss ASLey applauds your efforts to find out more about Deaf people and Deaf culture, even though it appears you got off on the wrong foot or should I say the wrong hand. Fortunately, your Deaf friend set you straight in a very direct way which is how Deaf culture works. Unfortunately, it left you reeling. So, I shall have to assume the role of the hearing-well-mannered person that you wished Janet could be and lead you to enlightenment.

"Deafness" has been the term used for hundreds of years to describe Deaf people in ways that, frankly, make my skin crawl. A specialist in "deafness" is a person who is primarily interested in one thing: How to "improve" Deaf people by restoring them to "hearing-ness." It probably does not occur to them that there are many Deaf people who have no desire to be "improved." These so-called experts perceive Deaf people as sad victims of hearing losses who will be grateful to anyone who can fix their supposedly tragic condition. Sort of like colonial Europeans who invaded the African and American continents with the goal of "civilizing" the native Africans and Americans or, failing that, eliminating them. So "deafness" clearly identifies someone with a "colonial" attitude toward Deaf people, even though they are happy and content to be Deaf. It is a loaded word with many negative connotations. The same is true for hearing-impaired. After all, would you, an ASL student, like to be labeled "signing-impaired"?

Enter "Deafhood" a term that Paddy Ladd, a British Deaf scholar invented in his trailblazing book "Understanding Deaf Culture: in Search of Deafhood." He defined Deafhood as a process by which Deaf individuals come to actualize their Deaf identity. In this process, Deaf people explore and discover the positive experiences of being Deaf, the rewards of using a natural visual language, the pleasures of expressing their unique cultural point of view, and many other positive aspects of life as Deaf people. They are ready and willing to defend their language and culture against "foreign" attacks by well-meaning (or not) hearing people.

My dear stunned student, perhaps you can understand why your Deaf friend Janet reacted so negatively to your use of the word "deafness." Be aware that "deafness" and "Deafhood" are antagonistic concepts which can hardly occupy the same sentence without causing a gnashing of Deaf teeth.

So, how can you get back in your Deaf friend's good graces? Perhaps you can buy Paddy Ladd's book and read it. It is not an easy read, so give yourself a few weeks or months. Be sure to carry it around with you wherever you go so that if you run into Janet, she'll see how you are trying to reform your attitudes and beliefs.

I make no guarantees that your friendship with Janet will be completely restored. Only time will tell. But, at least you and Janet will be on respectful terms again.

Mannerly,

Miss ASLey

SIGNS OF THE REAL WORLD

A STORY ABOUT A HEARING MOTHER, A DEAF SON, AND NATURAL DISASTERS

After all this work, it's time to enjoy a true story about a hearing mother who was overly worried about her Deaf son being killed by an earthquake. Perhaps you know of Deaf friends who have hearing families whose members might assume that their Deaf family members would be helpless in the face of some natural disaster. Nowadays, with all the technological advances, Deaf people are a lot safer but, even when these technologies had not yet been invented, Deaf people would be quite resourceful. Still, back in the 1980s, a hearing mother might be likely to worry about her Deaf son who moved to California, the land where the earth shakes, rattles, and rolls on various occasions. This story has not one, but two twists!! Watch MY ASL TUBE and enjoy:

MY ASL TUBE: 1-21: A HEARING MOTHER, A DEAF SON, AND NATURAL DISASTERS

Here are some questions about what happened in the story

1. What was Don's mother worried about after he moved to California? _____

   _____

   Do you think she was justified? _____

2. What event enabled Don to convince his mother to stop worrying? _____

   _____

3. What happened that made Don realize he needed to be alert to disasters?

   _____

4. How do you think Don and his mother might deal with future natural disasters? _____

   _____

   _____

DEAF CULTURE CORNER

THE DEAF PRESIDENT NOW MOVEMENT AT GALLAUDET UNIVERSITY

As we learned in *My ASL Book, Level 1*, ASL and Deaf culture began to be accepted and encouraged in educational programs across the United States from the 1960s onward. However, hearing people still controlled almost every aspect in the education of Deaf people. Among the more than sixty residential schools for Deaf children across the country, only three were headed by a Deaf director or superintendent. Additionally, less than ten percent of the teachers and administrators in all Deaf schools were themselves Deaf. The system tended to perpetuate itself because Deaf children attending these schools rarely encountered successful Deaf teachers and administrators and, consequently, their vision of their own possibilities pursuing careers in Deaf education became limited or nonexistent.

Hearing people literally ran the show and at the top of this pyramid of hearing-dominated education was Gallaudet University, "World's Only University for Deaf People." Gallaudet had been headed by a hearing president since its founding in 1864. The first four presidents of Gallaudet served long and successful terms: Edward Miner Gallaudet served for forty-six years (1864–1910) followed by Perceival Hall who served thirty-five years (1910–1945), followed by Leonard Elstad for twenty-four years (1945–1969) and Edward C. Merrill for 15 years (1969–1984). Each of these four presidents led the university to greater growth and success, contributing to the mystique that only a hearing person was suited to serve as the President of Gallaudet University.

Still, a number of Deaf leaders and their hearing allies felt that it was time that Gallaudet had a Deaf president at its helm. Even President Merrill voiced his support for such a possibility. Unfortunately, the Board of Directors, led by Jane Bassett Spillman, committed a series of incredible blunders which ultimately led the Gallaudet alumni, students, staff and faculty, and the national Deaf community to take matters in their own hands.

The first blunder of Spillman and her board was to ignore the requests by several Deaf leaders to consider including Deaf candidates in the search for the Gallaudet President. Instead, they selected Dr. Lloyd Johns as the fifth President of Gallaudet and announced his selection along with glowing superlatives about his leadership. A mere three months later, Dr. Johns resigned under a cloud of personal and professional issues. His resignation and the rumors about his shortcomings demolished the myth of the infallibility of a hearing Gallaudet President. Once again, Deaf leaders requested that Spillman and her board consider possible Deaf candidates in their search for the next Gallaudet President. Instead, the Board appointed Dr. Jerry Lee, Vice President for Administration and Business, to serve as Interim President. Then, a few months later, without any search for the best possible candidate, Deaf or hearing, the Board appointed Dr. Lee as the sixth President of Gallaudet. Many Deaf leaders were extremely disappointed at this turn of events.

Although Dr. Lee guided Gallaudet through a period of expansion and was instrumental in changing the college to a university, his presidency was cut short when he resigned to become a vice president for Bassett Furniture, a corporation that had been in Jane Bassett Spillman's family for generations and was currently headed by her husband. This glaring conflict of interest led many Deaf leaders to say, "Enough was enough!" A small group of these leaders declared that it was time for a Deaf president and the time was Now!! They began laying the groundwork for a campaign to convince the Board of Directors along with the students, faculty, and staff at Gallaudet University that a Deaf president was not a luxury but an absolute necessity.

They had their work cut out for them. Even after the board announced in February 1988 that three finalists had been selected and two of them were Deaf, many Deaf students and faculty members were ambivalent about the idea of a Deaf president of Gallaudet University. They felt that a hearing president would be better able to convince Congress to continue allocating funds that paid for seventy-five percent of the university's budget. Also, most of the past hearing candidates for Gallaudet's President had far more administrative experience than the Deaf candidates. The people who doubted the viability of a Deaf presidency failed to recognize that discrimination prevented most Deaf people from obtaining advanced administrative positions at Gallaudet and at other universities. They also failed to consider the fact that a Deaf candidate would be much more qualified to handle the unique issues and concerns of the Deaf and hearing members of the Gallaudet University community. Their knowledge and skills were badly needed to help Gallaudet succeed in its mission. Finally, Deaf students and leaders had never seen a Deaf person as president of a university, so no one had any idea of what it would be like.

When the Board announced that the three finalists were Dr. Harvey Corson, Deaf superintendent of the Louisiana School for the Deaf: Dr. I. King Jordan, Deaf dean of Gallaudet's college of arts and sciences; and Dr. Elizabeth Zinser, a hearing vice-chancellor of the University of North Carolina, a group of young Deaf leaders decided to try to change the Gallaudet Community's negative attitudes toward a Deaf president. They organized a rally held on May 1, 1988, and posted fliers around campus with the following thought-provoking words:

IT'S TIME!

In 1842, a Roman Catholic became president of the University of Notre Dame.

In 1875, a woman became president of Wellesley College.

In 1886, a Jew became president of Yeshiva University.

In 1926, a Black person became president of Howard University.

And in 1988, the Gallaudet University presidency belongs to a DEAF person.

To show OUR solidarity behind OUR mandate for a Deaf president of OUR university, you are invited to participate in a historic RALLY!

The organizers had expected to draw about 1,000 people to the rally. Instead, 1,500 people showed up. The rally moved through several different locations on the Gallaudet campus and nineteen Deaf leaders from the university and the national Deaf community exhorted the students, faculty, and staff to push for a Deaf president. "The Time is Now," they said. Their words inspired many people at Gallaudet to change their point of view and to support the selection of a "Deaf President Now"!

Many other Deaf individuals and organizations had been working behind the scenes to put pressure on the Gallaudet Board. Three national organizations, the Gallaudet University Alumni Association, the National Association of the Deaf, and the Fraternal Society of the Deaf had urged the Board to consider a Deaf president and had even contacted newspaper reporters and members of Congress about it. So, after the Wednesday, May 1 rally, people waited with a high degree of anticipation for the Board's announcement of the next President of Gallaudet University. The announcement had been set for Sunday, May 6 at 8:30 in the evening.

A large number of people traveled to the campus on Sunday night in anticipation of the announcement. When they arrived, they were stunned to discover that the Board had already distributed a press release two hours earlier announcing that the next President of Gallaudet University would be Dr. Elizabeth Zinser, the hearing candidate.

The shocked and enraged group of students, faculty, staff, alumni, and community members decided to march thirty-five blocks from the Gallaudet campus to the Mayflower Hotel where the Board had been meeting. There, the huge mob demanded that the Board President Jane Spillman come out and explain to them why she passed over two qualified Deaf candidates to select a hearing candidate with no experience in educating Deaf people. After a long wait, Ms. Spillman appeared but she was not able to explain to any satisfaction the decision of the board.

It turns out that the vote of the board had been ten to four in favor of Elizabeth Zinser. All of the ten votes in favor of Zinser were hearing and three of the four who voted for the Deaf candidate were themselves Deaf. So, there was a high degree of polarization even among the Board members. To make things worse, in the confusion during the aftermath of the Board's decision, Spillman was thought to have made the comment that "Deaf people are not ready to function in the hearing world." Spillman later denied making such a statement but the damage was done. In an age before the Internet, her comment "went viral" and placed Spillman and the Board in a tremendously unfavorable light in the eyes not only of the national Deaf community but also of the national and international news media and beyond them, people all over the world.

On Monday morning, May 7th, students chained shut all the entrance gates into the campus. Although most faculty and students were allowed to enter, members of the administration were not and the provost eventually had to declare the university closed.

Meanwhile, a delegation of ten students, two faculty, and two staff members presented a list of four demands to the Board:

1. The resignation of Elizabeth Zinser and the selection of a Deaf president
2. The resignation of Jane Spillman from the Board of Directors
3. An increase of Deaf board members until they reached a 51% majority
4. No reprisals against the protesters.

Unfortunately, after a prolonged discussion, the Board refused to accept any of the four demands.

That afternoon, Spillman and the board went to the Gallaudet field house to address a huge mass of Deaf and hearing students, faculty, staff, and alumni. Before Spillman could begin to speak, a Deaf faculty member Dr. Harvey Goodstein interrupted her, announced that the Board had refused to meet the four demands, and requested that everyone in the audience leave since there was no point in staying to listen to Spillman. In short order, Spillman and the board found they had no one to explain their decision to since the field house had emptied itself in a matter of minutes.

So commenced one of the most amazing weeks in the history of the Deaf world, second only to the arrival of Laurent Clerc and Thomas Hopkins Gallaudet and the founding of the first school for the Deaf back in 1817. It is impossible to describe all the events of that tumultuous week. You'll find a blow-by-blow account along with some great photos in Jack Gannon's "The Week the World Heard Gallaudet" or a detailed, incisive narrative in John Christiansen and Sharon Barnartt's "Deaf President Now." I can only give you some of the highlights:

Student support for the "Deaf President Now" movement crystallized around four student leaders, Greg Hlibok, president of the Student Body Government; Tim Rarus, past president; and Jerry Covell and Bridgetta Bourne, both student activists.

Elizabeth Zinser decided to come to Washington rather than stay in North Carolina until July when she was supposed to begin her term as Gallaudet's President. She was never able to set foot on the Gallaudet campus and had to conduct her campaign from off-campus headquarters. The students had hoped she would agree with their point of view; instead, at a press conference she announced, "I am in charge," dashing hopes for a resolution of the situation.

On Wednesday, May 9, Zinser, Greg Hlibok, and Marlee Matlin, an Oscar-winning Deaf actress appeared on ABC's *Nightline* to discuss the whole situation. At the end of the broadcast, Ted Koppel, the host of *Nightline*, asked Zinser if she was acting on her own or if she was a puppet of the Board.

World-wide support for the protesters continued to mount. Several members of Congress expressed their belief in a Deaf president and questioned Zinser's capability of managing Gallaudet because of her lack of knowledge about Deaf people and Deaf culture. The Deaf President Now movement raised tens of thousands of dollars in support of their campaign. More importantly, the faculty of Gallaudet University passed a resolution in support of the Deaf President Now movement. This was the last straw for Elizabeth Zinser. She knew she could not administer the college without the support of the faculty.

On Thursday, March 10, Elizabeth Zinser spoke just two words to Jane Spillman: "I resign." The protesters were ecstatic but this was only one-half of the four demands that they had made of the Board. So they continued to urge the adoption of the other three and a half demands.

On Friday, March 11, over 3,000 Deaf and hearing students, faculty, staff, alumni, and community members from all over the United States participated in a march on the U.S. Capitol. The march leaders carried a huge banner titled "We still have a dream," the same banner that civil rights leaders had used in a march to make Martin Luther King, Jr.'s birthday a national holiday. The march ended at the base of the capitol with multicolored flags and a huge "Deaf President Now" banner floating from the same platform where U.S. Presidential inaugurations had traditionally taken place.

Finally, on Sunday, May 12, the Board gave in and accepted all four demands and more!

> They selected I. King Jordan as the first Deaf president of Gallaudet University
> They agreed to increase Deaf representation on the Board to 51% or more
> They agreed not to institute reprisals against the protesters
> They accepted the resignation of Jane Bassett Spillman from the Board
> They then selected Philip Bravin as the new and Deaf Board chairman

What followed was a flood of celebrations at Gallaudet and in many other places in the U.S. The following week, the President of Gallaudet University, the chairman of the board, and the president of the Student Body Government had their first meeting. To their delight, they discovered that, for the first time in history, these three officers of "The World's Only University for Deaf People" didn't need an interpreter since they were all Deaf!

The protest was over but the Deaf community and the deaf educational system would never be the same. Students, faculty, staff, and community members in schools across the U.S. began to demand the same support for Deaf leadership and management of their educational programs. Within a few years after the Deaf President Now movement, the number of deaf superintendents in schools for the deaf had increased from three to seventeen. Eventually a sizeable percentage of residential schools and other educational programs were headed by Deaf or Deaf-sensitive individuals. A year later, the Americans with Disabilities Act was passed into law, some say, by the momentum generated by the DPN movement.

Even today, the DPN stands as a beacon for the advancement of Deaf people around the world.

You can enjoy an ASL version of the Deaf President Now Movement by a woman who was actually there!! As you watch, notice how the storyteller uses time transition signs to help the story flow smoothly.

MY ASL TUBE 1-22: THE DEAF PRESIDENT NOW MOVEMENT

HOW DID I DO?

I hope you enjoyed the information, games, exercises, and stories in this chapter. Now that you are in a better position to celebrate Deaf people, it's a good idea to check your progress in how well you were able to meet the goals for this chapter. Below are the goals along with a continuum from "I did great!" to "I need to work on this more." Write an "x" in the place that you feel reflects your progress in this chapter. You the student can say: "I have finished this chapter and now, I can":

1. Communicate information about various months and seasons.

   I need to work on this more   I did great!

2. Identify various holidays celebrated by both hearing and Deaf Americans and identify the month or months in which these holidays take place.

   I need to work on this more   I did great!

3. Describe various sports, hobbies, educational activities, places to go to, and other activities and destinations that Deaf people are involved in as a way to celebrate life or just to enjoy being with Deaf and hearing friends and families.

   I need to work on this more   I did great!

4. Communicate how you feel about various events and activities.

   I need to work on this more   I did great!

5. Use one of sixteen new adjectives to evaluate the quality of events and activities.

   I need to work on this more   I did great!

6. Identify and describe various Deaf holidays and celebrations on a local, regional, state-wide, and national level.

   I need to work on this more   I did great!

7. Use Non-Manual Markers as adverbs to describe how various actions were performed.

   I need to work on this more   I did great!

8. Describe the features of Deaf culture that demonstrate a "Deaf Gain" as opposed to a "Hearing Loss."

I need to work on this more   I did great!

9. Outline some of the benefits that Deaf people and Deaf culture can offer to hearing people and society in general.

I need to work on this more   I did great!

10. Identify or produce a variety of lexicalized finger-spelling signs and specify which parameter was changed to produce each sign.

I need to work on this more   I did great!

11. Describe the meaning of various coordinating conjunctions and use them to combine different pairs of ASL sentences.

I need to work on this more   I did great!

12. Outline the differences between "deafness" and "deafhood" perspectives.

I need to work on this more   I did great!

13. Narrate a story about earthquakes and tornados and misunderstandings between a hearing mother and her Deaf son.

I need to work on this more   I did great!

14. Narrate a brief history of the Deaf President Now movement and its impact on the power structure of the Deaf and hearing worlds.

I need to work on this more   I did great!

Visiting a Deaf Home

CHAPTER 2

INTRODUCTION TO THE CHAPTER

I hope you've been celebrating your friendships and interactions with Deaf people at various events both special and ordinary. If you haven't had much interaction, I hope you will have more opportunities soon to make friends and get involved with Deaf people. If you're nervous about being able to communicate in ASL with Deaf people, that's understandable. Your best bet is to pick activities and events where the stress level is not too high for you to handle. You might want to choose a low-stress situation where you'll only need to chat on a basic level and won't find yourself too embarrassed if you make mistakes. For example, you might attend a theater or film performance in sign language supplemented by voice interpreters. You'll be able to understand the show and also chat with Deaf people in the audience on a limited basis before or after the show or during intermission. Most of the time, Deaf people will be forgiving of your not-so-great signing skills.

Later, when you feel more confident, you might try a medium-stress event such as a service attended by Deaf people at a church, temple, or mosque. At such an event, you'll probably be expected to stay after the service and chat with the Deaf participants which means you'll need more ASL fluency in order to communicate with them. Other medium-stress events might include a Deaf dance (be sure to bring earplugs to protect you from the loud music), or a Deaf Halloween, New Years, Valentine's Day, or St. Patrick's Day party, or many other events and activities that you learned about in Chapter 1.

In this chapter, you're going to learn about a potentially high-stress activity—a visit to the home of a Deaf friend and his or her family. Since you'll be expected to chat in ASL on a personal level, you may feel that such a visit could be highly stressful. But, it doesn't have to be that way. If you adopt a higher tolerance for ambiguity and a relaxed attitude toward potentially embarrassing situations, you'll probably enjoy yourself regardless of what happens. At times, you may not have a clear idea of what is being communicated, but you can accept that you understand the gist of the conversation. If you commit a faux pas, just accept that you are human, forgive yourself for your mistake, and move on. At one time, I was like that; I got nervous about making mistakes when communicating with hearing people. But, after I got my PhD, I realized that one of the nice things about having an advanced degree was that, if you make an embarrassing mistake, people will assume you are "eccentric" rather than stupid. So, now, I have a relaxed attitude toward my stupid … er … eccentric mistakes!

In this chapter we'll help you develop the ability to participate in more intimate conversations with Deaf people in situations such as visiting the homes of Deaf people and their families. After you finish this chapter, you will be able to use ASL to:

1. **Share information about you and your Deaf friends in terms of where you and they are from or where you and they live now.**

2. **Produce or identify the name-signs for major cities in the USA.**

3. Produce or identify the signs for various conventional and unconventional dwellings that Deaf (and hearing) people live in.

4. Describe the various ways that Deaf (and hearing) people travel about, be it human power, horse power, public transportation, or unconventional means.

5. Given a tour of a typical Deaf home, describing the various rooms as well as the furniture and other objects within each room.

6. Produce the sign for any number from 1–10,000 or, given such a number, identify the number correctly.

7. Produce the sign for any amount of dollars or, given a specific amount of dollars, identify the amount which was given.

8. Participate in a dialogue about various items in the home, dealing with where they were bought, how much they cost, and whether the items were cheap, expensive, or reasonable in price.

9. Play a finger-spelling game involving categories.

10. Describe or identify various chores around the house, various day-to-day, or personal hygiene activities, and various meals and foods.

11. Produce or identify various events and activities that take place in a typical day in the life of a Deaf or hearing person.

12. Discuss the idea that a Deaf child can be a member of both its biological family and also the family comprised of Deaf community members.

13. Tell a joke about a tree that refused to fall down after it was almost completely chopped through by a lumberjack.

14. Discuss why many Deaf people do not believe they should be considered disabled.

15. Celebrate the life and pioneering achievements of Andrew Foster, Gallaudet University's first African American graduate.

THE CLASSROOM

THE DIFFERENCE BETWEEN "WHERE DO YOU LIVE?" AND "WHERE ARE YOU FROM?"

Before visiting your Deaf friends, you'll want some background information about them. For example, you'll want to know where they live and where they are from. These two questions have different meanings in Deaf culture (and probably hearing culture as well). If you ask Deaf people where they live, they will tell you the name of the town, city, or region where they reside right now. If you ask them where they are from, they will give you the name of the town, city, or region where they grew up or spent most of their lives. Or, they will tell you the name of the state where they attended a residential or mainstreamed school for the Deaf because their schools may have played a major role in their acquisition of ASL and Deaf cultural viewpoints. Sometimes the answer to "Where do you live?" and "Where are you from?" will be the same. In other words the Deaf person was born, went to school, and now lives in the exact same city.

But often, the answer to these two questions will be different. There are several reasons for this. First, Deaf people with hearing families may not have strong family ties, especially if the family members don't sign. So, Deaf people may be less concerned about maintaining family ties and less motivated to live in their family's hometown. Some may even move to a far-away town to "escape" a bad communication set-up.

Second, Deaf people may not be able to pursue career opportunities and find good jobs in the areas where they grew up, due to lack of educational programs that meet their needs or due to past job discrimination from businesses or agencies in these areas. So, they naturally seek employment in a more "deaf-friendly" city or region. I'm happy to report that this situation is improving, thanks to the Americans with Disabilities Act which prohibits educational and employment discrimination, and also, thanks to many new service agencies which have been established to meet the educational and career needs of Deaf people.

Finally, there may not be many Deaf people in a particular town or city, so the Deaf person will move away from his or her hometown to a different city with a larger Deaf community. Usually, Deaf newcomers are easily integrated into this new community.

One other reason for Deaf mobility is college and university programs with large numbers of Deaf students such as Gallaudet University, NTID, California State University, Northridge, and many others. Deaf students at these programs come from all over America and they share with each other a multiplicity of ideas, experiences, and information about their home states and hometowns. Based on what they learn from the "mixing bowl" experience, Deaf students may decide to move on to a new city or state after they graduate. To give you an example, a Deaf woman, whom we will call Abby, grew up in Wyoming which has no residential school for the Deaf. Instead, she attended mainstreamed schools and then enrolled at Gallaudet University. Her career goal was to teach theater and dance to Deaf children, but, after she graduated, she found that there were no jobs for Deaf teachers in any of the mainstreamed schools in her state. Additionally, she made many new friends from Northern California and decided to accept a position at the California School for the Deaf to teach drama in the high school department.

Naturally, if you express an interest in where your Deaf friends live or are from, they'll be happy to share their memories, experiences, and insights with you. Watch MY ASL TUBE and learn how you can ask these questions. Remember, in "Wh" questions, the "Wh" word is usually last.

MY ASL TUBE 2-1: "WHERE DO YOU LIVE?" AND "WHERE ARE YOU FROM?"

Here is what you saw on MY ASL TUBE:

| You | live | where? |

You   are from   where?

NAME-SIGNS FOR MAJOR U.S. CITIES

Now that you know how to ask your Deaf friends where they live or where they are from, we'll teach you the name-signs for some of the major cities in the United States. Almost all have their own unique name-sign, so learning them all might seem overwhelming. However, most name-signs follow fairly predictable forms. You should be able to figure things out with a little practice. We can't include the name-signs of every city in *My ASL Book*, so you need to ask your ASL instructor for the signs for the cities and towns in your area.

Being able to participate in a conversation about where you or your Deaf friends live or are from can improve your rapport with them, since you will be sharing great memories and experiences.

Here are some general rules for name-signs for various cities:

1. Signs for cities with two-word names tend to use the first letter of each word (but not always). For example, Kansas City, Las Vegas, Long Beach, Los Angeles, Sacramento (S-a-c), San Diego, San Francisco, and San Jose all have name-signs based on their initials.

2. Name-signs for some cities are made by forming the finger-spelled first letter of a city and sweeping the hand in a horizontal and then a vertical movement that looks like a large "7." Don't ask me why—it's just a signing convention. The cities of Austin, Boston, Chicago, Detroit, Indianapolis, Philadelphia, Rochester, and Tucson are signed this way.

3. Some city name-signs are made by forming the finger-spelled first letter of a city and then slightly shaking the handshape sideways or up and down. The signs for Columbus, Ohio; Denver, Colorado; Fresno, California (forward and back); Knoxville, Tennessee; Louisville, Kentucky; and Seattle are made this way. The sign for "Baltimore" is made with the "B" handshape moving up and down with the palm oriented to the left and fingers facing forward. The sign for "Phoenix" is made with an "X" instead of a "P." What's with Phoenix? My theory is that the sign for "dry" is made with an "X," so the sign for "Phoenix" reflects this. But that is just my theory.

4. Some city name-signs are made by tapping on a part of the body: Dallas (on the temple), Houston (on the chin), Fort Worth (on the non-dominant hand), Atlanta (left and right sides of the chest), and Cleveland (same as Atlanta). Sliding signs include Memphis and New Orleans (with an "O" or "F"), both of which slide along the non-dominant hand in two repetitive motions.

5. Name-signs for some cities are based on characteristics of the city. So, "Washington" is signed with a "W" spiraling out from the shoulder that simulates the epaulets of General Washington's uniform; "Nashville" uses an "N" handshape in the sign for "government" (since Nashville is the capitol of Tennessee); "El Paso" is made by the movement of an "E" moving through a "pass" formed by the "L"; (since "El Paso" means "a mountain pass"); "New York" is made with a "Y" sliding on flat "B" hand like a train passing back and forth; and Saint Louis starts with an "S" handshape, then traces an arch and ends with "L" to simulate the famous St. Louis arch. And, in almost every region, any city or town with a large proportion of rich people will be signed using the first letter of the city's name and brushing upward on the nose (as in "snooty").

6. Probably the most fascinating name-signs for cities are those that used to be the name-sign of a person that lived in that city. For example, the residential school for the Deaf in Minnesota is located in the small town of Faribault, quite some distance from Minneapolis. One student who attended the Faribault school was from Minneapolis and his name-sign was a "D" tapping on the left side of the chest. So, whenever people talked about "Minneapolis," instead of spelling the name of the city, they would sign "D-on-the-chest's city." Gradually, the sign for "Minneapolis" became abbreviated to "D-on-the-chest," even though there is no "D" in the word "Minneapolis." This happened for other cities as well, including Pittsburgh, Pennsylvania (F-brushing down the left chest), San Antonio, Texas ("G" - tapping the side of the chin), Milwaukee ("G" sliding sideways on the chin), and other cities. Fascinating!!

7. As a general rule, if a few Deaf people live in a specific town or city, there won't be a name-sign for it. Instead the name will be finger-spelled. As more and more people move into a these towns or cities, name-signs will eventually be invented.

In the next MY ASL TUBE, you'll see all the signs for cities that we discussed here.

MY ASL TUBE 2-2: THE SIGNS FOR VARIOUS CITIES IN THE UNITED STATES

There are a lot of signs for cities, so we'll give you a practice exercise to help you develop your skill in remembering city name-signs. In MY ASL TUBE, we'll show short conversations that show the name of a Deaf or hearing person and where that person is from. On the next page, you'll find a map of the U.S. which includes all the major cities. You will need to write the name of the person next to the correct city on the map. For example, you'll see a woman who will say: "Hello, my name is Abby and I am from Chicago." Based on this conversation, you need to write "Abby" next to "Chicago" on the map.

Not only will this "game" help you recognize all the name-signs for cities, but you'll also re-learn all the places you learned about in your fifth-grade geography class and forgot as you got older!!

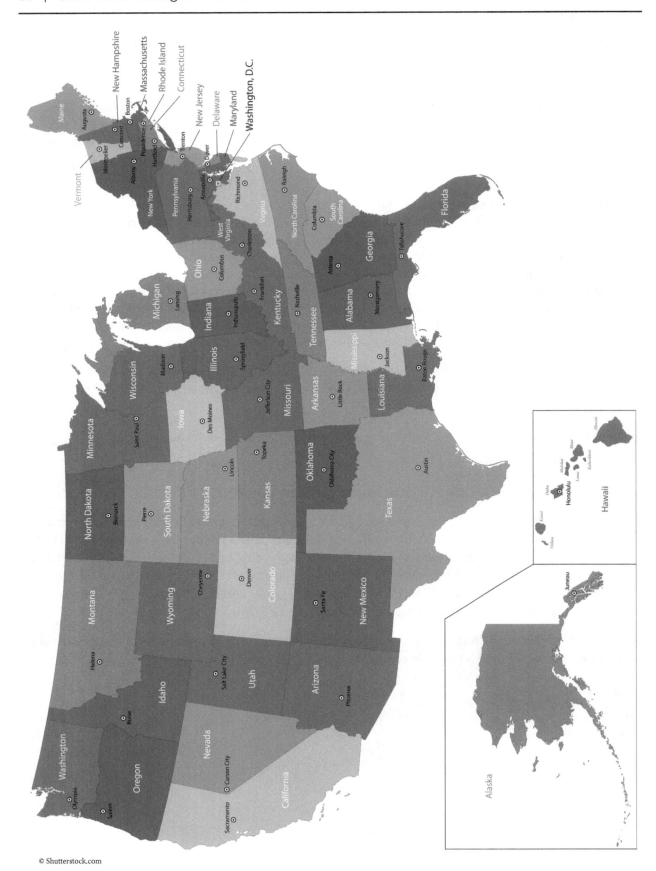

MY ASL TUBE 2-3: THE "WHERE ARE YOU FROM?" MAP GAME

FINDING OUT WHAT KIND OF HOMES YOUR DEAF FRIENDS LIVE IN

Since you're going to be visiting Deaf friends and families, you'll need some idea of what kind of dwelling they live in. Not only will this help you find their home, but you'll also have an inkling of their lifestyles. All you need to do is ask, "Do you live in a house or an apartment or what?"

You may be surprised at some of your friends' answers. Sometimes Deaf people like to joke about things such as the kind of place they live in. They might say, with a chuckle, "I live in a shack!" or "I live in my car." On second thought, I have known Deaf people who were so poor that they actually lived in a VW Bus, an RV, a teepee, and other unconventional dwellings for months and even years. Let's watch MY ASL TUBE and learn about the kinds of dwellings that Deaf and hearing people live in:

MY ASL TUBE 2-4: KINDS OF DWELLINGS

Here are the signs you learned about in MY ASL TUBE:

CONVENTIONAL DWELLINGS:

For some dwellings, we finger-spell the whole name or an abbreviation of the name:

apartment = a-p-t	cabin = c-a-b-i-n	condominium = c-o-n-d-o
dormitory = d-o-r-m	motel = m-o-t-e-l	townhouse = t-h

For other dwellings, we have signs:

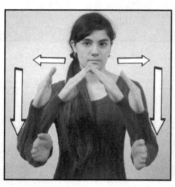

house

hotel

trailer

UNCONVENTIONAL DWELLINGS: Like signs for conventional dwellings, we use a mix of finger-spelled abbreviations and signs to indicate various unconventional dwellings. Here they are:

Barn = b-a-r-n   Teepee = t-e-e-p-e-e   RV = r-v

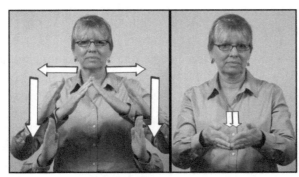

houseboat

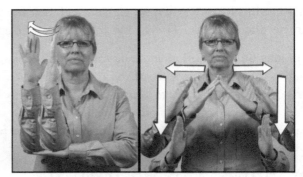

tree house

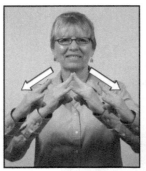

tent

shack

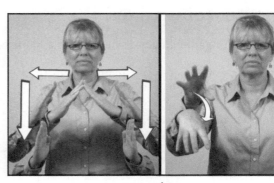

mansion

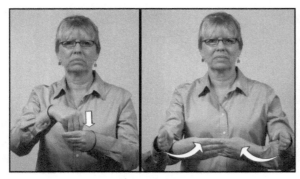

in a box

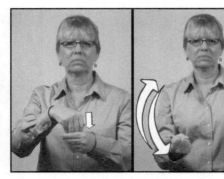

in a car

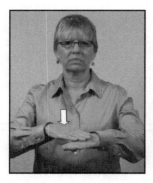
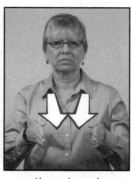

| on | the street | under | a bridge |

Let's practice identifying the various places that Deaf people live in (or say they live in). In the next MY ASL TUBE, you'll meet a variety of people who will give you their names and tell you what kind of dwelling they live in. Write the name of each person's dwelling below:

1. _____
2. _____
3. _____

4. _____
5. _____
6. _____

7. _____
8. _____
9. _____

10. _____
11. _____
12. _____

13. _____
14. _____
15. _____

16. _____
17. _____
18. _____

19. _____
20. _____
21. _____

MY ASL TUBE 2-5: DO YOU LIVE IN A HOUSE, APARTMENT, OR WHAT?

Here is another way to practice your newly learned signs. On the next page, you'll find a chart with pictures of various dwellings. In MY ASL TUBE 2-6, you'll meet some Deaf people who will tell you their names and what kind of dwelling they live in. Write the name of each person in the box with the correct dwelling.

MY ASL TUBE 2-6: DEAF PEOPLE AND PLACES THEY LIVE IN

FINDING OUT ABOUT WAYS THAT DEAF (AND HEARING) PEOPLE TRAVEL ABOUT

You'll also want to learn some signs for modes of transportation. After all, if you're going to visit Deaf friends and their families, how will you get to their homes? Additionally, if your Deaf friends visit you, it would be a good idea to know what kind of transportation is available to them. I have a very good friend who, as a matter of principle, does not own a car. He lives in the San Francisco Bay Area which has lots of public transportation choices. But, when he makes plans, he needs to make adjustments for his lack of a car. So, you need to know what travel modes your Deaf friends have access to. But watch out. Deaf people may make jokes or try to pull your leg about what kind of transportation they use.

There are many questions you can ask to find out how Deaf people travel about. For example:

1. How will I go to your home?

2. How do you commute to work?

3. How do you go to school?

4. We'll meet at the restaurant. How will I go there?

There are many more possible questions, but for now, we'll focus on these four. In the next MY ASL TUBE, you'll learn how you can sign these questions.

MY ASL TUBE 2-7: ASKING HOW DEAF PEOPLE TRAVEL

Now you know how to ask questions about how your Deaf friends get around from home to work, school, and other places. If you ask them, what do you think will be their responses? Let's learn signs for modes of transportation, private and public, conventional and unconventional.

MY ASL TUBE 2-8: WAYS THAT PEOPLE TRAVEL

Here are some of the ways that Deaf (and hearing) people travel as shown in MY ASL TUBE:

HUMAN POWER

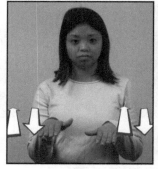
walking

bicycling

rowing a boat

running

rollerblading

skateboarding

HORSEPOWER

driving

riding in a carpool

riding a motorcycle

PUBLIC TRANSPORTATION

riding in a vehicle . . .

bus

train

fingerspell t-a-x-i

taxi

flying

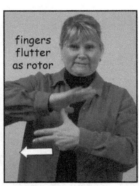

fingers flutter as rotor

going by helicopter

fingerspell f-e-r-r-y

going by ferryboat

UNCONVENTIONAL

horseback riding

horse and carriage

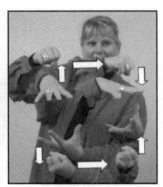

Star Trek transporter

Let's practice identifying the various ways that Deaf people travel (or say they travel). In the next MY ASL TUBE, you'll meet a variety of people. They'll give you their names and tell you what kind of travel they use for various situations. On the next page, you'll find a chart with pictures of various modes of travel. Write the name of each person in MY ASL TUBE in the box with the correct mode of travel.

MY ASL TUBE 2-9: ASKING DEAF PEOPLE HOW THEY TRAVEL

THE DEAF COFFEE HOUR

LEARNING SOME NEW SIGNS IN A TOUR OF A DEAF HOME

Now that you can find out where a person lives and how to get there, you're ready for a visit to a Deaf person's home. Let's imagine that you've developed a great friendship with a woman named Mary and she invites you to her home for lunch. You already know she lives in San Francisco in a house and you can get there by car or bus. So you and Mary make plans and one day you drive to the city, ready to make a first visit to a Deaf person's home.

Sometimes, when people visit a Deaf home, their host may give a tour of the household and Mary is no exception. She gives you "the grand tour" of her house, showing off the various rooms and the furniture and fixtures in each one. Watch the next MY ASL TUBE as Mary shows you around her house. You may recognize some of the signs from the campus tour in Chapter 3, but you'll also learn a lot of new signs. So, be prepared to remember them all.

MY ASL TUBE 2-10 A TOUR OF A DEAF PERSON'S HOME

That was quite a tour of Mary's house, wasn't it! Did you learn a lot of new signs? You may already know some of the signs for the various rooms and objects in her house. Also, for some objects, you will need to finger-spell the name. Here are all the signs you saw during Mary's tour.

KITCHEN (there are two signs for this room)

Finger-spelled names: stove, ref (for refrigerator), oven, sink, blender, dishwasher

Signs you already know: table, chair, shelves, coffee maker, microwave, plant

New signs:

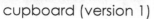

cupboard (version 1)   cupboard (version 2)   dishwasher

refrigerator   toaster

BATHROOM (has the same sign as "toilet")

Finger-spelled names: Sink, rug, tub; *Signs you already know:* Toilet, Mirror, Plants

New signs (you will learn a lot of other new bathroom signs later in the chapter):

towel   toilet paper   soap   make-up

OFFICE (You already know this sign)

Signs you already know: desk, chair, computer, laptop

LIVING ROOM OR DEN

Finger-spelled names: den, sofa, VCR, DVD, AC, TV, Stereo, Rug, hassock

Signs you already know: pictures, plant, coffee table, grandfather clock

New signs:

living room (vers. 1)

living room (vers. 2)

lamp

plush chair

rocking chair

curtains

Venetian blinds

fireplace

sliding door(version 1)

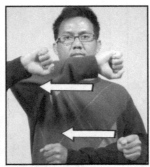

sliding door(version 2)

portable fan

ceiling fan

BEDROOM

Signs you already know: chair, mirror, lamp

New signs:

dresser bed king-sized queen-sized

double twin alarm (with) flashing light

OTHER PLACES

Finger-spelled names: yard, patio, porch, attic

Signs you already know: office, library

New signs:

outside inside swimming pool

laundry room   garage   basement

You'll want to practice using all the signs you learned. Work with a classroom or a Deaf friend. Compare notes about your homes with each other. This is a fun way to practice these signs and also to satisfy your curiosity about your friend or partner's home!

What you do have	What your friend/partner has	What you don't have

Kitchen

_____	_____	_____
_____	_____	_____
_____	_____	_____

Bathroom

_____	_____	_____
_____	_____	_____

Office

_____	_____	_____
_____	_____	_____

Living room/Den

_____	_____	_____
_____	_____	_____
_____	_____	_____

Bedroom

_____	_____	_____
_____	_____	_____
_____	_____	_____

Other places

_____	_____	_____
_____	_____	_____
_____	_____	_____

FINGER-SPELLING FINESSE

Let's learn how to communicate about another important subject: Money! You'll discover that most Deaf people have a relaxed attitude about the cost or value of things they see in a house. If a Deaf friend has a new television, it's quite natural to ask him or her how much it cost and where it was purchased. So let's expand our repertoire of number signs for and then learn how to use these signs to talk about money matters.

NUMBERS FROM 1–100

Let's learn some more numbers so you can communicate with Deaf people about practical problems involving money. When you chat with Deaf people about something you bought, they will often ask you how much these items cost. They're not being nosey. They just need useful information for future purchases. After all, Deaf people miss out on a lot of information on the radio and television, so your sharing of this kind of information will help them shop more effectively and economically.

You already know how to sign 1–50, so let's learn how to sign 51–100.

MY ASL TUBE 2-11 SIGNS FOR NUMBERS FROM 51–100

Did you notice something interesting about the signs for 67–69, 76, 78–79, 86–87, 89, and 96–98? They all have a twisting motion. If the first digit in the number is lower than the second digit (e.g., 67, 68, 69, 78, 79, 89), you twist upward from the lower number to the higher number. If the first digit in the number is higher than the second digit (e.g., 76, 86, 87, 96, 97, 98), you twist downward from the higher number to the lower number. It seems complicated, but just think, "digits go up—twist up; digits go down—twist down." Watch MY ASL TUBE 2-12 to see how this works.

MY ASL TUBE 2-12 "TWIST" NUMBERS

It would be a good idea to practice these numbers from 1–99. One way is to work in pairs. One partner signs a number and the other writes it down; then they switch. Or you and your Deaf and hearing friends can get together and play a game of Buzz. You can find the rules for the game in Chapter 4 of *My ASL Book, Level 1*.

HUNDREDS FROM 100–900

Let's learn the signs for numbers in the hundreds. They are based on the old Roman numeral system. "100" in Roman numerals is "C," so the sign for "100" is "1 C," for "200," "2 C," for "300," "3 C," and so on. It's quite simple. However, due to a process of assimilation between the numbers and "C," the signs for "200," "300," "400," and "500" have two forms: a long form that is used in formal situations and a shorter more informal sign. Watch MY ASL TUBE to learn more about how these numbers are signed.

MY ASL TUBE 2-13: SIGNS FOR "HUNDREDS"

Here are the signs you learned in MY ASL TUBE

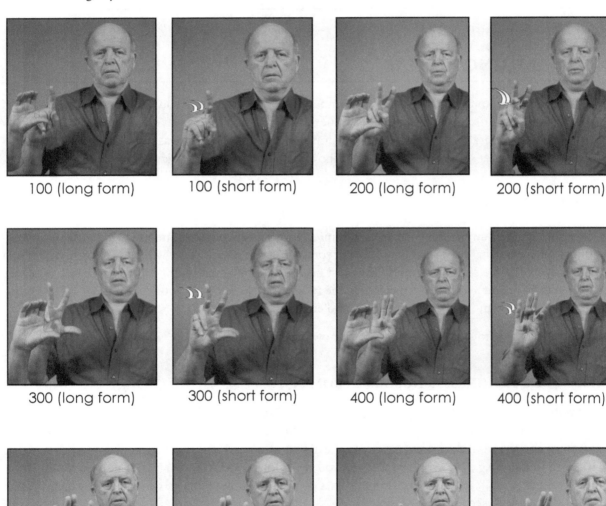

| 100 (long form) | 100 (short form) | 200 (long form) | 200 (short form) |

| 300 (long form) | 300 (short form) | 400 (long form) | 400 (short form) |

| 500 (long form) | 500 (short form) | 600 (long form) | 600 (short form) |

We'll give you a short practice exercise to help you remember all the numbers you learned in MY ASL TUBE. You'll see signs for various multiples of a hundred. Write them down below.

A. _____; B. _____; C. _____; D. _____; E. _____;

F. _____; G. _____; H. _____; I. _____; J. _____

MY ASL TUBE 2-14: PRACTICE EXERCISES FOR NUMBERS 100–900

How was that? I hope you got your numbers right.

NUMBERS FROM 1–10,000

Now you know 999 new signs!! You can easily sign the numbers from 1–99. For the numbers 100–999, all you have to do is combine the "hundreds" sign with the numbers 1–99.

Here is a challenging practice exercise. In the next MY ASL TUBE, a signing performer will produce the signs for any number from 1–999. Write the correct number in the blanks below:

A. _____; B. _____; C. _____; D. _____; E. _____;

F. _____; G. _____; H. _____; I. _____; J. _____;

K. _____; L. _____; M. _____; N. _____; O. _____

MY ASL TUBE 2-15: PRACTICE EXERCISE FOR NUMBERS 1–999

What about numbers over 999, such as 1,000, 3,000, 10,000, and so on? Remember how we used the Roman numeral "C" to indicate hundreds? We use the Roman numeral "M" to indicate thousands. In the early versions, the dominant hand "M" tapped the palm of the non-dominant hand "B." But, gradually, the sign became more streamlined and, instead of using an "M," Deaf people now use a bent "B" handshape. Watch MY ASL TUBE and you'll learn how it is done.

MY ASL TUBE 2-16: SIGNS FOR THOUSANDS

Now practice with a partner, using the numbers from 1,000–9,999. One partner signs a number and the other writes it down; then they switch. Practice and practice until you can comfortably read or produce any number between 1 and 9,999.

TALKING ABOUT BUYING AND SELLING THINGS

Deaf people will frequently talk about the prices of things they bought. This information-sharing aspect of Deaf culture helps them make informed choices about things they're planning to buy.

If you want to chat with Deaf people about the prices of things, you need to know the signs for various denominations of dollars and cents. For now, we'll focus on the signs for dollars. Denominations from $1 to $10 have similar sign forms: the signer produces the number of the denomination and then twists his/her hand in a clockwise direction. For denominations of $11 and up, a signer produces the number plus the sign for "dollar." Please watch MY ASL TUBE to see how you make the signs for various dollar denominations.

MY ASL TUBE 2-17: SIGNS FOR VARIOUS DOLLAR DENOMINATIONS

Now that you know how to produce and read signs for various denominations, you can chat with your Deaf friends about different furnishings, where they got them, and how much the furnishings cost. Let's go to MY ASL TUBE and learn some new signs you can use for chatting with Deaf friends about these topics.

MY ASL TUBE 2-18: SIGNS USED TO CHAT ABOUT HOW MUCH THINGS COST

Here are the responses to some of the questions that were asked in MY ASL TUBE:

1. **IS IT NEW?**

old

used

new

2. WHERE DID YOU BUY IT?

Signs you already know or can finger-spell: friend; give-me; free; store; thrift store (finger-spell "Thrift"); flea market (spell "flea" and "market")

New signs:

Internet   auction

3. HOW MUCH DID YOU PAY? HOW MUCH DID IT COST?

New signs:

pay   cost   free   cheap

reasonable   about right   expensive

Now we'll have some fun visiting Mary's house. You can follow along and watch Mary and Judy chatting about Mary's furnishings. For each object, Mary and Judy will discuss several things: the name of the object; how old or new the object is; where Mary got the object from; how much the object cost and whether the object is free, cheap, expensive, or just right. Watch MY ASL TUBE and fill out the form below:

#	Object	Old? New?	Where acquired?	Cost?	Expensive? Cheap?
1.	_____	_____	_____	_____	_____
2.	_____	_____	_____	_____	_____
3.	_____	_____	_____	_____	_____
4.	_____	_____	_____	_____	_____
5.	_____	_____	_____	_____	_____
6.	_____	_____	_____	_____	_____
7.	_____	_____	_____	_____	_____
8.	_____	_____	_____	_____	_____
9.	_____	_____	_____	_____	_____
10.	_____	_____	_____	_____	_____
11.	_____	_____	_____	_____	_____

MY ASL TUBE 2-19: TALKING ABOUT VARIOUS ASPECTS OF HOME FURNISHINGS

Congratulations! You've increased your skill in chatting with Deaf people about their favorite possessions and how your friends acquired them.

AT THE ASL CLUB

TALKING ABOUT ROUTINES

Now that we can use ASL to chat about various rooms in Mary's home and the furnishings found in these rooms, let's learn how to chat about the day-to-day routines of Mary's family. She is married to Bill, a Deaf man who teaches math at a school for the Deaf. They have two children, Tracy, a Deaf girl aged 12, and Loren, a hearing boy, aged 8. We already know the signs for morning, noon, afternoon, evening, and so forth. We can use these and other signs to chat about a family routine.

Many of the activities you reviewed in Chapter 1 can be part of a family routine. Additionally, the family routine will include not-so-fun activities known as:

CHORES AROUND THE HOUSE

Watch MY ASL TUBE and learn the signs for various chores

MY ASL TUBE 2-20: CHORES AROUND THE HOUSE

Here are some of the signs you learned in MY ASL TUBE:

cleaning   sweeping   vacuuming   washing windows

dusting   washing the car   doing laundry   cooking

washing dishes   giving dog a bath

mowing the lawn

taking care (of pets, babies, etc.)

babysitting

loafing

studying

staying home

Now work with a partner. Take turns discussing each chore and tell your partner how you feel about the chore. Perhaps you detest mowing the lawn but enjoy staying home. You and your partner can make a list using the form below. Each partner can make a "profile" of the other partner in terms of things he/she likes or hates and share the profile with the class.

Here is the form:

Your Chore   How you feel about it   Partner's Chore   How he/she feels about it

1. _____   _____   _____   _____

2. _____   _____   _____   _____

3. _____   _____   _____   _____

4. _____   _____   _____   _____

5. _____   _____   _____   _____

6. _____   _____   _____   _____

7. _____   _____   _____   _____

8 _____   _____   _____   _____

9. _____   _____   _____   _____

10. _____   _____   _____   _____

11. _____　_____　_____　_____

12. _____　_____　_____　_____

13. _____　_____　_____　_____

14. _____　_____　_____　_____

DAY-TO-DAY AND PERSONAL HYGIENE ACTIVITIES

In addition to all the chores that people do at home, we'll learn the signs for other day-to-day activities as well as hygiene activities. Watch MY ASL TUBE:

MY ASL TUBE 2-21: DAY-TO-DAY AND PERSONAL HYGIENE ACTIVITIES

Here are the activities that you learned about in MY ASL TUBE.

DAY-TO-DAY

Waking up—Deaf people:

waking up

alarm

flashing light

bed vibrator

Waking up—hearing people:

alarm clock

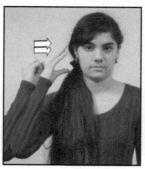
rings-in-my-ear

clock radio

rooster

Waking up and morning routine—Deaf and hearing people:

(wake up) myself

(someone) wakes
me up

get up

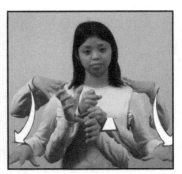

get dressed

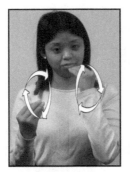

eating

breakfast

making lunch

kissing

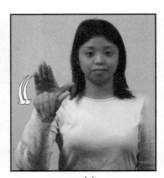

good bye

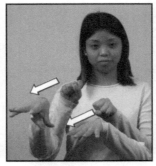

dropping off . . .
kids at school or day
care

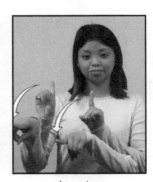

going to . . .
work or school

Afternoon and evening routine—Deaf and hearing people:

picking up (kids)

arriving

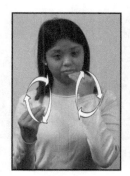
eating

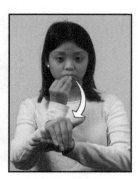
dinner

 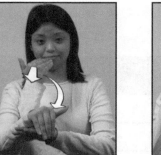
kissing good night

getting into bed

falling asleep

PERSONAL HYGIENE

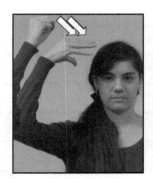
showering

bathing

brushing teeth

shaving (female)

shaving (male)   trimming a beard   applying deodorant

You can practice these new signs by working with a partner and comparing each other's day-to-day and personal hygiene activities. Look at each activity and decide if this is something you do routinely. Fill out the form below.

MY ROUTINE   **MY PARTNER'S ROUTINE**

I do this activity	I don't do this activity	He/she does this activity	He/she doesn't do this activity

FOODS

There is one more area where we'll learn some new signs: what people eat during their daily routine. Watch MY ASL TUBE to learn the signs for basic foods.

MY ASL TUBE 2-22: FOODS

Here are all the signs you learned in that MY ASL TUBE:

BREAKFAST

Finger-spelled words: oatmeal, bagel, pancakes, waffle, yogurt, omelet

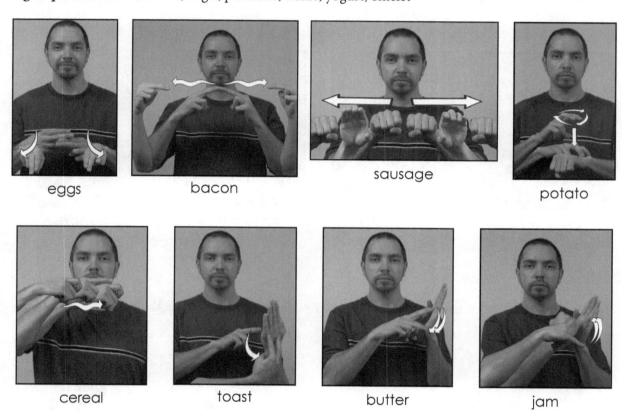

eggs   bacon   sausage   potato

cereal   toast   butter   jam

LUNCH

Finger-spelled words: Jello, chips, junk, names of candy, cookies, etc.

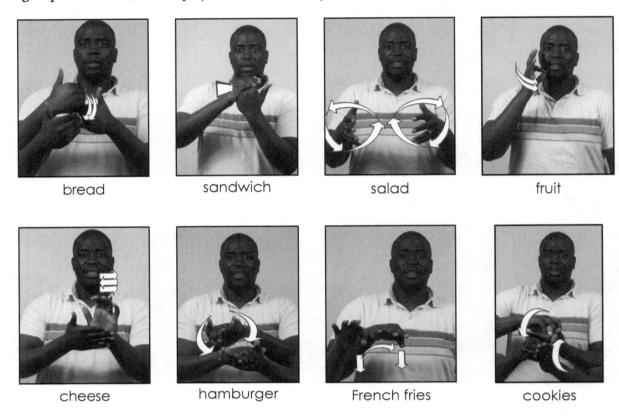

| bread | sandwich | salad | fruit |
| cheese | hamburger | French fries | cookies |

DINNER

Finger-spelled words: Beef, ham, steak, pork, beans, peas, pasta, berries, rice, cake.

| vegetable | meat | chicken | fish |

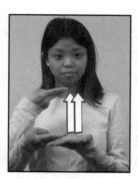

| spaghetti | soup | pie | ice cream |

Now meet with a partner and share food preferences with each other. Use the form on the following page. Write in each food choice based on preferences. If the partner really likes the food choice, list it close to the smiley; if not list it close to the frowny. Here is dialogue:

Partner A: *(food choice), you like?*   Partner B: *Respond*

Partner B: *(food choice), you like?*   Partner A: *Respond*

. . . and so on.

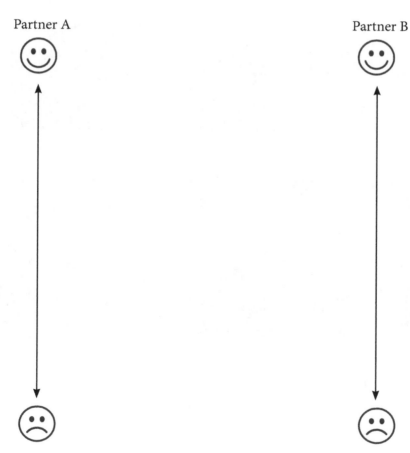

Based on the food choices on this form, each partner creates a profile of the other partner's food preferences and shares this with the class. Partners can also list additional food choices and ask for the signs for these food choices.

TIME TRANSITIONS

Suppose you are visiting a Deaf home and chatting with your Deaf host Barb. Perhaps you might ask Barb, "How was your day?" Barb, naturally would give you a rundown of what happened to her all day. Let's watch as Barb tells us what she did all day. But, before you do this, you need to learn some of the transition signs that she will use to show the time order of the events. There are three signs she will use. Watch MY ASL TUBE to learn these three signs.

MY ASL TUBE 2-23: SIGNS FOR TIME TRANSITIONS

Here are the some of the transitional phrases you can use to introduce a new event. For example, "at eight o'clock ... I had breakfast." Or "At about 8 o'clock ... I read the newspaper." And so on. Here are the most commonly used transitional phrases:

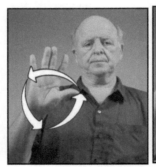

At eight o'clock . . .   At around eight o'clock . . .

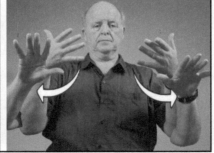

After I finished showering ("shower finished") . . .   A little later . . .   much later . . .

Now we're going to watch the conversation where Barb tells us about her day. Please fill out the following chart, listing each event and the time (exact or approximate) that it happened.

WHAT TIME? (EXACT/APPROX.)	A.M. EVENT	WHAT TIME? (EXACT/APPROX.)	P.M. EVENT
_____	_____	_____	_____
_____	_____	_____	_____
_____	_____	_____	_____
_____	_____	_____	_____
_____	_____	_____	_____
_____	_____	_____	_____
_____	_____	_____	_____

MY ASL TUBE 2-24: BARB'S DAY

Were you able to list all the events and times for Barb's Day? I hope so. If you're not sure, go back and review all the signs in Barb's story.

Now, we're going to meet Joan, a Deaf woman who is a bit of an oddball. She'll tell you all about her day. Please fill out the following chart, listing each event and the time (exact or approximate) that it happened.

WHAT TIME? (EXACT/APPROX.)	A.M. EVENT	WHAT TIME? (EXACT/APPROX.)	P.M. EVENT
_____	_____	_____	_____
_____	_____	_____	_____
_____	_____	_____	_____
_____	_____	_____	_____
_____	_____	_____	_____
_____	_____	_____	_____
_____	_____	_____	_____

MY ASL TUBE 2-25: JOAN'S DAY

What about your own daily routines? Are they like Barb's or Joan's? Let's work in pairs. You can tell your partner your routines and then let your partner tell you his or hers. Write down the routines and the times in the following chart and compare your routines. Later, in class, you can share with your classmates which of you and your partner's routines are similar and which are different. Here's the chart.

WHAT TIME? (EXACT/APPROX.)	**YOUR EVENTS**	**WHAT TIME?** (EXACT/APPROX.)	**PARTNER'S EVENTS**
_____	_____	_____	_____
_____	_____	_____	_____
_____	_____	_____	_____
_____	_____	_____	_____
_____	_____	_____	_____
_____	_____	_____	_____
_____	_____	_____	_____

Now, we're going to try to guess the morning routine of a mysterious gentleman. Let's watch a video and decide. What do you think he does first? Second? Third? Below is a mixed-up list of events in his morning routine. Write the numbers 1, 2, 3, 4 … To show the order of the man's events. For example, you might write in #1 next to "The alarm rings," #2 next to "He wakes up," and so on. Okay? Let's go ahead!

THE MYSTERIOUS GENTLEMAN'S ROUTINE:

_____ He puts his alarm clock in water.

_____ He gets dressed.

_____ His alarm clock rings.

_____ He cuts his nose hairs.

_____ He brushes his teeth.

_____ He gets up.

_____ He shaves.

_____ He remembers his dentist appointment.

_____ He makes the bed.

_____ He runs to his car.

_____ He wakes up.

_____ He burns his toe with some hot water.

_____ He bangs his head against the wall.

_____ He exercises.

_____ He drives his car to the dentist.

_____ He hangs up his alarm clock to dry.

_____ He tucks in his teddy bear.

Now, watch MY ASL TUBE to find out if you guessed the correct routine for the man.

MY ASL TUBE 2-26: THE MYSTERIOUS ENGLISH GENTLEMAN'S DAY

How did you do on this exercise? Not what you expected, was it?! Work with your partner to get the correct order of events in the routine that you saw on MY ASL TUBE.

ASK MISS ASLEY: THE DEAFINITE ANSWER

(Miss ASLey is a Deaf professional etiquettarian. In other words, she feels it is her duty to remind various uninformed people whenever they make a Deaf cultural faux pas, and to show them the proper cultural behavior to exhibit toward people in the Deaf world. If you want to learn how to show proper humility toward Deaf people, Miss ASLey is the person you need to ask.)

Dear Miss ASLey,

I am a hearing ASL student. For my ASL class, I am required to do a "field trip" to a Deaf community event. Since I am a Christian, I decided to attend a Deaf church service, near my home. The service was to be conducted in ASL by a Deaf minister. I thought how wonderful it was that the minister could inspire Deaf people to become better Christians.

When I arrived at the Deaf church, I found that I did not know anyone, so I sat quietly in a pew, focusing on my religious thoughts. The service had not started and everyone was chatting in sign language. I enjoyed the quiet, although some Deaf people were joking and their laughter disturbed the atmosphere of religious solemnity. It seemed so rude! But it did not seem to bother the minister and his assistant who were sitting by the church altar.

Suddenly, my solemn thoughts were disturbed by a loud noise from the back of the church. A white-robed lady walked down the aisle banging on a huge drum. It turned out she was the choir leader. The other choir members followed her down the aisle up to the front of the church. There they sang one of my favorite hymns. But the banging of the drum, the out-of-rhythm signing of the hymn and the out-of-tune voicing by the interpreter really disturbed me. I wanted to stick my fingers in my ears but I was afraid it would offend people. They might even throw me out of the church.

Then the service began. The bible reading was nice but the old man who was reading the bible kept stopping to read each passage and then sign it to the congregation. I wondered why he could not practice in advance so the reading would be smooth and inspiring. Then there was another banging, out-of-rhythm, out-of-tune performance by the choir! I sat on my hands to avoid putting them to my ears.

Finally the Deaf minister got up and delivered his sermon. I am used to a solemn and formal church service so the minister's sermon was a little too casual for my taste. Then, right in the middle of the sermon, one of the people in the congregation got up, waved for attention, and asked the minister to please explain one of his points again, more clearly. And the minister went right ahead and re-delivered part of his sermon.

Miss ASLey, I was shocked!!! I was raised to believe that a church is a House of Worship and that people are supposed to follow proper decorum. In my church, no one would dare interrupt the minister when he was giving a sermon. NO ONE! It is just NOT DONE!

Shouldn't someone teach the church members "normal" behavior in a church? Like being quiet before the sermon, avoiding loud noises like a drum, practicing bible reading, sitting quietly during the sermon, and so on. That would make their church more solemn and religious and more suitable for a Christian service.

A Signing Christian

Marilyn Damon

***

Dear Ms. Damon,

First of all, Miss ASLey commends you for taking on the huge challenge of attending a Deaf church service. This can be an intimidating experience because of the high potential for making a faux pas and suffering painful humiliations. It speaks well of your courage that you would try to participate in a Deaf church service on your own without any guidance from a Deaf friend.

On the other hand, your becoming upset because the Deaf church did not conform to a "normal" religious service speaks more of your naiveté and ignorance of Deaf culture. What is "normal" anyway? In a Deaf church, you would most likely be the abnormal one and, while that situation might be uncomfortable, it would give you an opportunity to learn what is really involved when Deaf people come together for a religious experience.

The choir experience certainly would not be all that appealing to a hearing person such as yourself because it doesn't sound like a traditional church music. But it makes sense to a Deaf congregation in terms of a visual and tactile experience. The drumbeat provides a musical coda for people who cannot hear even though it might be disturbing to hearing people. Likewise, the signed song would feel strange to a hearing person because it uses a different tempo and rhythm that is suited more for Deaf eyes than for hearing ears. The odd bible reading is another example of how Deaf people adjust their religious experiences. A hearing bible reader would keep his or her eyes focused on the bible while speaking the passage to the audience. However, a Deaf bible reader needs to maintain eye contact with the congregation, so he or she can only deliver a few lines of the bible after which he or she must look down and read the next part of the bible passage. Finally, the Deaf man who got up in the middle of the sermon to ask a question was just trying to gain a clearer idea of what the minister had been saying. Many Deaf people are not afraid to ask questions even in potentially intimidating situations. On the other hand, many hearing people are afraid to ask questions in this situation. Someone jokingly told me that hearing children learn to stop asking questions by the age of seven. What a pity!

So, Marilyn, when you visit the Deaf church again, offer up a prayer of thanks for the unique ways that Deaf people worship the Divine.

Religiously Culturally Deaf Yours,

Ms. ASLey

SIGNS OF THE REAL WORLD

It's time for another joke, this time about a mysterious tree that refused to cooperate with a lumberjack who was trying to chop it down.

MY ASL TUBE 2-27: THE TREE

Now that you enjoyed the joke, please try to tell the joke yourself to a classmate or to your class as a whole. Don't forget to use direct address as the narrator and role-shift as the characters of the lumberjack and the tree doctor. Also, be sure to use any classifiers you found in the story such as the ENTITY classifier for the tree and the HANDLE classifier for the axe and other instruments.

DEAF MYTHBUSTERS

A sizeable portion of the Deaf community does not believe that Deaf people are handicapped or disabled, and prefer being called Deaf rather than "hearing-impaired." Most hearing people would consider deafness a handicap or a disability and prefer to use the term "hearing-impaired" instead of Deaf because it sounds more neutral and less tragic. Who's got it right?

In Chapter 1, we learned the difference between Deaf people (capital D) and deaf people (lower-case d). The former group includes Deaf people who use ASL and participate in their own cultural milieu while the latter group includes people with hearing losses who may or may not use ASL. This includes a large group of people who have lost their hearing due to advancing age.

Deaf and deaf people comprise a sizeable and diverse group. The population of the Deaf World is, according to the best estimates, 600,000 people. If we expand this to the population of all deaf people, it's about three million and if we expand it further to include hard of hearing people, the total is about twenty-five million people. So, it's important that we use accurate and up-to-date terms lest we be accused of "cooking" the statistics.

First of all, let's look at the issue of whether or not we should refer to people who can't hear very well, as "hearing-impaired." I'm going to turn the tables on you, the ASL student. How would you like it if Deaf people referred to you as "signing impaired" or "manually retarded"? Doesn't give you the warm fuzzies, does it? So, you can understand why Deaf people do not like to be referred to as "hearing-impaired." Very likely, hard of hearing people don't like to be referred to as "hearing-impaired" either. So, instead of using a blanket term "hearing-impaired" for some twenty-five million people with a hearing loss, let's be more sensitive and just call them deaf and hard of hearing people. For those who use ASL, just call them Deaf people.

While we're on the subject of terminology, two other terms that you may encounter in television and print media are "deaf-mute" and (less common) "deaf and dumb." The latter term used to mean a person who was deaf and also could not speak but in modern usage, the word "dumb" refers to lack of intelligence as in the film "Dumb and Dumber." Deaf people react to "Deaf and dumb" as fighting words in the same way that African Americans react to the "N" word.

Also, Deaf people react negatively to the term "deaf-mute" because it implies that they are helpless losers without a shred of communicative ability. But, just because Deaf people cannot hear does not mean that they cannot make use of their vocal abilities. In fact, a popular game in some residential schools is a contest to see which student can shout the loudest. The contestants position themselves facing the corners of a room (for maximum effect) and, at a cue, scream their lungs out. Believe me, you would not want to be in the room when the contest was going full blast because the noise level would probably render you deaf. As you can see, people who use the terms "deaf and dumb" and "deaf-mute" are not only offending Deaf people but they will need a reality check. If you encounter someone using these terms, please set them straight. And if, heaven forbid, you see the terms used in a newspaper or magazine, write a letter to the editor explaining that these terms are offensive to Deaf people.

Of course you might be challenged by someone who says, "Well they still can't talk, can they?" The answer is that most Deaf children must take speech lessons during their school years whether they want them or not. So most Deaf people can talk but it's a big question about whether or not their speech can be understood. There are many stories about Deaf people whose speech teachers told them they spoke beautifully but, were completely humiliated when they discovered that store clerks, wait-people, doctors, nurses, and all sorts of hearing people could not understand them. Many of them opted to never communicate via speech again. Consequently, a large proportion of Deaf people prefer to communicate via other means such as gesturing or writing back and forth on a notepad. If they use speech at all, it's only with people who know them well such as close friends and family members. So, to answer your friends' challenges, you might say that some Deaf people can talk but not everyone understands them.

Next, let's address the issue of whether or not Deaf people consider themselves handicapped or disabled. First of all, the term "handicapped" has gone out of favor due to the mistaken idea that it implies a person who cannot work and goes begging with "cap in hand." It suggests someone who is totally helpless and needs to subsist on handouts. Instead, the preferred term for people with physical, mental, emotional, and sensory impairments is "disabled" or even "differently-abled."

Do Deaf people consider themselves disabled? Let me tell you a story about something that happened to me a few years ago. I was a member of the Berkeley City Commission on the Disabled and I happened to mention this to my Deaf friend who I will call Sandeep. He was a well-educated Deaf man who had a PhD in Educational Administration from Gallaudet University. When I mentioned that I was a member of this Commission on Disability, he was incredulous. "But you're not disabled," he said. "You can work, you have a job, you get along in life just fine. Why do you call yourself disabled?" This kind of reaction is very common among Deaf people. Many of them do not accept being lumped together with people who have physical or mental disabilities.

Here's another story for you. I will call it the Deaf people vs Chinese people Paradox. Tell me what you think. An elderly Chinese couple moved from China to San Francisco to live closer to their three adult children, all of whom were naturalized U.S. citizens. The Chinese couple moved into a house in Chinatown and had no difficulty adapting to their new life in a foreign country. They shopped at Chinese grocery stores, ate at Chinese restaurants, went to Chinese clubs to socialize and play cards, and otherwise lived in a completely Chinese environment where they never had to speak a single word of English. On the few rare occasions when they had to interact with English-speaking Americans, the couple would take one of their children with them to interpret between Chinese and English. Needless to say, the Chinese couple was perfectly comfortable in a Chinese environment and never had a need to use English. Would you consider this Chinese couple disabled? Probably not.

Now consider a retired Deaf couple who live a mile or so away from the Chinese couple in a neighborhood of mostly hearing people. The couple almost never had any interaction with their hearing neighbors. Instead, they traveled great distances to visit Deaf friends, to participate in dinners out with other Deaf people, to attend Deaf events where they socialize and play cards with Deaf friends, and to live almost completely apart from the hearing public. When they needed to interact with hearing people, they used a personal or a video relay interpreter or resort to writing back and forth. Sometimes, if hearing family members knew signs, the Deaf couple might ask them to interpret for them. The Deaf couple's way of life is almost exactly the same as that of the hearing Chinese couple. You can't call the hearing Chinese couple disabled, so, by the same token, how can you apply the label "disabled" to the Deaf couple?

Most Deaf people consider themselves an ethnic or cultural minority similar to Asian Americans, Hispanic Americans, or African Americans. That is because they use a different language, marry other Deaf people, participate in extensive Deaf family and school networks, and support a vast array of Deaf organizations with social, political, economic, recreational, and other interests. Nonetheless, Deaf people do not entirely reject working with the disabled community. Many state associations as well as the National Association of the Deaf (NAD) have worked with various disability groups to get laws passed protecting the rights of disabled people. The NAD has been instrumental in promoting federal legislation such as the Americans with Disabilities Act (ADA), the Individuals with Disabilities Education Act (IDEA), and other vital federal laws and regulations that have improved the lives of disabled people tremendously.

Perhaps it is time for hearing people to stop pointing their fingers at Deaf people and asking, "Are you a culture or a disability group?" Instead, let's point to the larger hearing community and ask: "Are you a 'Deaf-friendly' community or are you a community full of access barriers against Deaf people?" If Deaf people are really "disabled," it's because the larger hearing community disables them by erecting and maintaining barriers that block their access to vital services and information.

Consider this: What if everybody was Deaf and there were no hearing people in the world? In this context, Deaf people would not be disabled at all. They would go about their lives, attending school, getting married, pursuing a career, raising children, getting old, and retiring without any real difference from hearing people with one exception: They would communicate all their needs either via sign language or via some sort of written language. No one would be "disabled."

But, when Deaf people compare this "non-disabled" society with the one we live in today, where a large percentage of the population is hearing, they find a huge problem: a sizeable majority of information is communicated to the public via speech and hearing. As a result, Deaf people are denied access to tremendous amounts of information that their hearing counterparts take for granted. To make things worse, the larger hearing majority tends to apply negative labels to Deaf people due to their reliance on sign language as a means of communication. It never crosses their mind that hearing people are just as disabled due to their dependence primarily on speech and hearing. So, let's dispense with the label "disabled" and look at some of the barriers that prevent Deaf people from getting the information and support they need. Here are a few:

COMMUNICATION BARRIERS: As we learned in Chapter 1, speech and lip-reading are poor communication modes for Deaf people because only about thirty percent of speech sounds are visible on the lips. The solution to this communication barrier is to provide alternate means of visual communication for Deaf people. There are many possibilities:

1. Providing sign language interpreters when needed.

2. Hiring Deaf people or hearing people who are sign-skilled to be service providers in a variety of roles, be they coffee baristas, school teachers, police officers, doctors and nurses, or any other occupation.

3. Offering print or electronic text information as a fallback for everything that is communicated through speech and hearing. Some examples of this include captions for various films, television, and theater programs and scripts for lectures and tours in museums, as well as service persons who are able to patiently write out information on a notepad, whiteboard, electronic tablet or other media.

INFORMATION BARRIERS: Most deaf and hard of hearing students grow up in "information poor" environments. Their parents and family members usually cannot sign, and these students have no access to radio programs and have only limited access to television and film programs (although this situation has improved tremendously in the past fifteen years). Due to ineffective educational programs, they are often left with reading skills too weak for understanding books and print media. Additionally, they are almost never exposed to Deaf adult role models, so they have a limited vision of their possibilities for success in academic and career fields. There are many solutions for these information barriers:

1. Encouraging and supporting efforts by family members to learn ASL and to include their Deaf family members in various family activities.

2. Providing effective bilingual instruction to Deaf and hard of hearing students in both ASL and English.

3. Developing innovative programs to expose Deaf children to Deaf role models. For example pairing hearing and Deaf families to get together frequently for social events.

ATTITUDE BARRIERS: Our society tends to hold either of two viewpoints about Deaf people. The first, sometimes called the deficit or pathological viewpoint, holds that deaf people suffer from a hearing impairment and the goal of their upbringing and education is to help them overcome this pathology. Solutions for this deficit include training in speech and lip-reading, medical interventions, surgery, and other actions designed to transform Deaf people into copies of hearing people. This "deafness as deficit" approach has proven tremendously damaging to the social and psychological well-being of Deaf people sometimes with extreme results. I know of at least five Deaf persons who could not "make the grade" as hearing people and committed suicide.

The second viewpoint about Deaf people holds that they have a unique language and culture, and the goal of their upbringing and education is to maximize their skill in this language and culture, as well as to educate them about the language and culture of hearing people. Some research has shown that this cultural perspective produces a higher level of success among Deaf people. This perspective needs to be communicated to a wide variety of Deaf, hard of hearing, and hearing people including school personnel, hearing students, potential employers, and other members of the hearing and deaf public.

One final point: when we speak of communication, information, and attitude barriers, the lack of access works both ways. Deaf people are denied access to the information and support they need for success in the world of Deaf and hearing people; hearing people are denied the information and support for learning about an ethnic minority with a huge potential to widen their understanding of what it means to be human.

LINGUISTIC ILLUMINATIONS

NOUN AND VERB PAIRS

As you interact with Deaf people and develop greater skill in communicating in ASL, you've probably started noticing many of the unique features of this visual language. In this second ASL book, we can only touch upon a few linguistic features. As you progress through higher levels of ASL, you'll begin to develop an intuitive sense of how this language is structured.

For example, you may have noticed that some nouns and verbs are very similar in handshape, location, and orientation but differ in movement. Let's look at some examples of this kind of noun-verb pair:

MY ASL TUBE 2-28: SOME NOUN-VERB PAIRS—SINGLE MOVEMENT VERBS

What did you notice about noun-verb pairs? Yes, right, the noun sign is made with two short movements in the same direction while the verb sign is made with just one movement. Now, you'll see a series of signs on MY ASL TUBE. Write down whether the sign is a noun or a verb and what it means. Then see if you can create the other member of the noun-verb pair. Finally, write down what you think is the meaning of this other member. We have done the first one for you.

Sign	Noun or Verb?	Meaning?	Other Member of Noun-Verb Pair
1.	*noun*_____	*plant*_____	verb: *to grow*_____
2.	_____	_____	_____
3.	_____	_____	_____
4.	_____	_____	_____
5.	_____	_____	_____
6.	_____	_____	_____
7.	_____	_____	_____
8.	_____	_____	_____
9.	_____	_____	_____
10.	_____	_____	_____

MY ASL TUBE 2-29: IDENTIFYING NOUN-VERB PAIRS—SINGLE MOVEMENT VERBS

How did you do with this challenging exercise? As you can see, ASL has some remarkable linguistic features that can help you understand and communicate in this visual language.

Most verbs that represent a single event are usually signed with a single movement. But not all verbs signify a single movement. For example, the sign for the verb "riding a bicycle" uses a classifier to mimic the action of peddling a bicycle. The verb for "to ride a bike" makes three or more large circular motions while the noun for "bicycle" makes just two tightly controlled circles. Watch the next MY ASL TUBE and you'll see other examples of noun-verb pairs where the verb is signified by three or more repetitive motions.

MY ASL TUBE 2-30: NOUN-VERB PAIRS—REPETITIVE MOVEMENT VERBS

Did you notice the difference between the nouns and the verbs in each pair? Now, let's see how good you are at recognizing a noun or a verb in a noun-verb pair where the verb has repetitive movements. This can be quite challenging but I'm sure you'll do great. You'll see a series of signs on MY ASL TUBE. Tell whether the sign is a noun or a verb and what it means. Then see if you can create the other member of the noun-verb pair. Finally, write down what you think is the meaning of this other member. We have done the first one for you.

Sign	Noun or Verb?	Meaning?	Other Member of Noun-Verb Pair
1.	*verb*_____	*to sing*_____	noun: *music*_____
2.	_____	_____	_____
3.	_____	_____	_____
4.	_____	_____	_____
5.	_____	_____	_____
6.	_____	_____	_____
7.	_____	_____	_____
8.	_____	_____	_____
9.	_____	_____	_____
10.	_____	_____	_____

MY ASL TUBE 2-31: IDENTIFYING MEMBERS OF NOUN-VERB PAIRS—REPETITIVE MOVE-MENT VERBS

DEAF CULTURE CORNER: DEAF HEROES AND SHE-ROES

ANDREW FOSTER: DEAF AFRICAN AMERICAN PIONEER

A popular website has called Andrew Foster "The Gallaudet of Africa." However, I like to think he was actually "the Laurent Clerc of Africa" for many reasons. Like Clerc, Foster was a Deaf man with strongly held beliefs about how education could liberate Deaf people. Almost exactly one hundred and forty years after Clerc set sail for America, intent on using education to transform the lives of Deaf Americans, Andrew Foster flew to Africa intent on the same deeply held belief and goal.

Foster was born in 1925 in Ensley, Alabama, a small suburb of Birmingham, which was then a center for the iron and steel industry. His father was a coal miner who did his best to support his family, despite limited financial circumstances. At the age of eleven, Andrew and his younger brother both became infected with Spinal Meningitis which caused them to become totally deaf. Since there were no educational opportunities for Deaf children in their area, the family sent the two brothers to the Alabama School for Colored Deaf in Talladega, about fifty miles from home. The Deaf brothers did the best they could but, unfortunately, the quality of education at the segregated school was quite poor. However, the family moved to Michigan when Andrew was sixteen, and he and his brother enrolled in the Michigan School for the Deaf where their educational prospects improved.

Andrew wanted to attend Gallaudet College, the "World's Only College for the Deaf," but his educational background was not yet adequate for him to succeed in college. So he took a correspondence course with the American School in Chicago and graduated in 1951. The much-improved education enabled him to gain acceptance at Gallaudet which had never previously enrolled an African American student. Andrew Foster became the first Deaf African American to graduate from this prestigious college (now a university). Foster later went on to complete two Master's degrees at other colleges. He clearly valued education as a path to greatness.

Foster lived and breathed strong spiritual values. His family was very religious and they attended church regularly. One weekend, a missionary from Jamaica visited Foster's Sunday school class and shared his experiences while working in Africa. Foster was inspired by the missionary's achievements and felt that he too could become a missionary someday.

Unfortunately, when the Deaf African American graduate of Gallaudet tried to secure support for becoming a missionary to Deaf Africa, he encountered almost complete resistance. The missions he contacted were not only racist, but also could not imagine a Deaf man succeeding on a continent where education of Deaf children was almost non-existent.

In response, Foster decided to set up his own mission, the Christian Ministry of the Deaf (CMD), in 1956. He traveled to Africa for the first time in 1957 and found mind-boggling obstacles. Most of the hearing African missionaries he encountered told him that there were no Deaf people in their area. Many people held a common belief that deafness was a curse so families hid their deaf children or left them in the wild where they perished from exposure or from animal attacks. When Clerc came to America in 1817, he encountered an entire population that did not believe Deaf people could be educated; likewise Andrew Foster found that almost all Africans did not believe an education was possible for Deaf African children.

Against these obstacles, Foster struggled to establish programs that would educate and nourish the hearts and minds of Deaf children in Africa. When he learned about a community in Ghana that had large numbers of Deaf children, due to hereditary factors, he decided to set up a Deaf school there. He had no funds to build such a school, but Foster conducted after-school classes for Deaf children, using classrooms in schools for hearing children. Remember all the discouraging remarks by the hearing African missionaries who said there were no Deaf children? In a short time, over 300 families contacted him, asking him to enroll their Deaf children in his school.

Andrew returned to the United States and proceeded to raise funds for a permanent residential school for Deaf children. Finally, he returned and established the first school for the Deaf in Africa in Nigeria. For the next three decades, Foster and his organization, the CMD founded thirty-one schools for Deaf children in thirteen countries: Benin, Burkina Faso, Burundi, Cameroon, Central African Republic, Chad, Democratic Republic of Congo, Gabon, Ghana, Ivory Coast, Nigeria, Senegal, and Togo. They also established a number of churches, Sunday schools, youth camps, and teacher-training facilities for Deaf people. Some of the schools that Foster and CMD founded were later taken over by government or private agencies. As the news of the success of these schools spread throughout Africa, more and more countries established schools for Deaf children. For all his wonderful work, Andrew Foster was awarded an Honorary Doctorate in Humane Letters by Gallaudet University in 1970.

Andrew met and fell in love with a German Deaf woman named Berta who also believed in Foster's spiritual and educational mission. They were married in Nigeria and continued to work for education of the Deaf in Africa. Andrew and Berta Foster had five children of their own. Unfortunately, Berta contracted cancer in 1975 and, because the nomadic life was causing difficulties for her health, the family moved back to the U.S. Andrew began to spend half of the year in the United States raising funds and the other half in Africa, organizing and promoting educational programs for Deaf Africans.

Sadly, his thirty years of service to the Deaf people of Africa came to an abrupt end in 1987. Foster was trying to travel to another school and was "lucky" to secure the last seat available on a flight. But the plane crashed in Rwanda, killing all aboard.

At the memorial service and later at the dedication of the Andrew Foster Theater at Gallaudet University, a parade of Deaf African leaders gave testimony about how Andrew Foster transformed their lives and the lives of Deaf Africans everywhere. Even today, Foster's organization the CMD continues the work begun by this "Father of Deaf Education in Africa."

Let's enjoy this story in ASL about the life of Andrew Foster.

MY ASL TUBE: 2-32: THE STORY OF ANDREW FOSTER

HOW DID I DO?

I hope you enjoyed all the things you learned in this chapter. You can use your new skills and knowledge to interact comfortably with Deaf people in their homes and in other places of friendship and good will. It's a good idea to check your progress. Below are the goals for the chapter along with a continuum from "I did great!" to "I need to work on this more." Write an "x" in the place that you feel reflects your progress in this chapter.

Now that you have finished Chapter 2, you, the student, can use ASL to:

1. Share information about you and your Deaf friends in terms of where you and they are from or where you and they live now.

    ⟵───⟶

    I need to work on this more   I did great!

2. Produce or identify the name-signs for major cities in the USA.

    ⟵───⟶

    I need to work on this more   I did great!

3. Produce or identify the signs for various conventional and unconventional dwellings that Deaf (and hearing) people live in.

    ⟵───⟶

    I need to work on this more   I did great!

4. Describe the various ways that Deaf (and hearing) people travel about, be it human power, horsepower, public transportation, or unconventional means.

    ⟵───⟶

    I need to work on this more   I did great!

5. Given a tour of a typical Deaf home, describing the various rooms as well as the furniture and other objects within each room.

    ⟵───⟶

    I need to work on this more   I did great!

6. Produce the sign for any number from 1–10,000 or, given such a number, identify the number correctly.

    ⟵───⟶

    I need to work on this more   I did great!

7. Produce the sign for any amount of dollars or, given a specific amount of dollars, identify the amount which was given.

    ⟵───⟶

    I need to work on this more   I did great!

8. Participate in a dialogue about various items in the home, dealing with where they were bought, how much they cost, and whether the items were cheap, expensive, or reasonable in price.

    ←───→

    I need to work on this more   I did great!

9. Play a finger-spelling game involving categories.

    ←───→

    I need to work on this more   I did great!

10. Describe or identify in ASL, various chores around the house, various day-to day or personal hygiene activities, and various meals and foods.

    ←───→

    I need to work on this more   I did great!

11. Produce or identify various events and activities that take place in a typical day in the life of a Deaf or hearing person.

    ←───→

    I need to work on this more   I did great!

12. Discuss the idea that a Deaf child can be a member of both its biological family and also the family comprised of Deaf community members.

    ←───→

    I need to work on this more   I did great!

13. Tell a joke about a tree that refused to fall down after it was almost completely chopped through by a lumberjack.

    ←───→

    I need to work on this more   I did great!

14. Discuss why many Deaf people do not believe they should be considered disabled.

    ←───→

    I need to work on this more   I did great!

15. Celebrate the life and pioneering achievements of Andrew Foster, Gallaudet University's first African American graduate.

    ←───→

    I need to work on this more   I did great!

CHAPTER 3

Deaf People Have Two Families

INTRODUCTION TO THE CHAPTER

As you may recall from Chapter 4 of *My ASL Book, Level 1*, one way you can become close to Deaf people is to chat and share information about each other's families. That way, you can learn a lot about the family life of your Deaf friends and how it affects their personal and cultural view of the world.

However, when you try to chat with Deaf friends about their families, you may sometimes feel like you are stepping through a minefield. That is because there are some serious communication problems in families where your friends may be the only Deaf family member. About ninety-five percent of Deaf people have hearing parents and siblings and approximately seventy percent of these hearing family members do not know or use American Sign Language.

Shocking, but true.

Additionally, many hearing members of these families view being deaf as a tragic medical condition and can only see a dark future for their Deaf family members. Many hearing relatives of Deaf people have only a limited understanding of how being a part of the Deaf community and participating in a Deaf culture can be an inspiring and enriching experience. In a few of these families, a hearing brother or sister may pick up some sign language skills and cultural knowledge and consequently develop a stronger bond with the Deaf family member. But, for the majority of hearing families, Deaf people are deprived of communication, understanding, and support within their hearing families.

So, don't be surprised if some of your Deaf friends tell you that they either have no contact with their families of origin or they limit their visits to formal family events such as holiday gatherings, weddings, or funerals. Some have described a family visit as a "three-day hurry-up-get-it-over-with visit." When the Deaf person first arrives, the hearing family gathers around to catch up on news. The Deaf family member will try to communicate about what has been happening in his or her life, either by writing, or by laboriously speaking and lip-reading. After an hour or so, the Deaf person and his family will have become exhausted by the struggle to communicate. The hearing family members will resume talking among themselves, leaving the Deaf family member out in the cold.

Some will try to give an occasional running summary of what the family is talking about for the benefit of the Deaf family member. But it will be awkward and far from adequate. Pretty soon, the Deaf family member will ask to be excused and go off to read or watch TV. If the Deaf family member brings a Deaf spouse to the family visit, the Deaf couple will begin chatting with each other in a separate conversation which the hearing family members cannot understand since they don't know sign language. It is as if an invisible wall has sprung up between the hearing and Deaf family members.

More and more frustrated, the Deaf family member begins a count-down toward the end of the three-day visit—"Only two more days," "Only one more day," "Only four more hours,"—until the longed-for departure happens and, with a sigh of relief, the Deaf family member says good-bye. The hearing family members feel guilty about their lack of connection, but they don't know how they can make this work. During the whole visit, he or she has simply gone through the motions of being part of a family without actually being included which is intensely unsatisfying.

You may ask, "If this is such a frustrating situation, why don't the hearing family members learn to sign?" There are many factors that prevent them from doing so. The main reason is that they receive poor advice from doctors as well as audiologists, speech pathologists, and many other speech-and-lipreading-"ologists" who are devoted to "repairing" broken Deaf people. These specialists are almost always not qualified as child development specialists or educators, but they assume they have the right to give out advice to families even though that advice has a negative impact on the communicative and educational development of Deaf family members.

Often, their advice is based on myths passing as "facts." For example, they may say that, if families use sign language, the Deaf family member may never learn to speak. WRONG! Research has consistently shown that learning a sign language supports and enhances a Deaf person's development of speech. Or they may say, "Speak slowly and clearly and your child will lip-read you and understand you." WRONG! Only about thirty percent of speech sounds are visible on the lips which means that lip-reading is basically a guessing game. But Deaf children have only a limited repertoire of English words or no words at all, so how are they to guess the correct words? Over and over again, this harmful advice has ruined any chances of healthy and fulfilling relationships between hearing and Deaf family members. There ought to be a law banning medical and "ology" professionals from advising family members about the best educational and communicative choices available to them.

The harmful advice of these professionals is not the only problem. In addition, hearing family members have difficulty accepting and celebrating the unique nature of their Deaf family members. Virtually every response to the expression "My child is deaf," is either "I'm so sorry!" or "Don't worry! You can get a cochlear implant and your child will hear again!" What about this response: "Your child is Deaf? Wow! That must be exciting! You can learn so much from Deaf people about communicating through vision and gesture! I would love to visit with your child!" That kind of response would be so much better than the typical bombardment of sympathy and bad advice and the horror stories about the epic struggle they will face in transforming their son or daughter into a "normal" child. When hearing families buy into this tragic view, it's not surprising that their Deaf family member wants to limit family time as much as possible.

On the other hand, if hearing family members develop good sign language skills, show understanding and acceptance of the Deaf experience, and maintain a positive attitude toward Deaf culture and Deaf community, their Deaf family members will thrive. A lot of research has shown that, when deaf children are exposed to a bilingual environment of ASL and English at birth or early in life, they will progress in their academic and social development at about the same level as hearing students.

Despite the difficulties that some of your Deaf friends will experience with their hearing family members, they are able to enjoy a much better communication situation once they start their own families. That is because most Deaf people marry or become partners with other Deaf people or with hearing people who have good ASL skills. These spouses or partners model effective communication approaches for their children, whether these children are Deaf or hearing. Such a family can be a wonderful support for every Deaf individual.

Hearing children of Deaf adults must deal with both Deaf and hearing worlds. Many call themselves CODAs (Children of Deaf Adults) and they form a unique group within the Deaf community. They even have their own local, regional, national, and international organizations. They need support because they must cope with the Deaf world at home and the Hearing World at school. This is especially true if they are the targets of bullies or insensitive classmates and teachers.

Deaf people have one additional choice in the diversity of friends, communities, and organizations. They develop an extensive network of friends and associates which they use to create an extended "second family" of Deaf, hearing, and CODA people. Through numerous opportunities to get together, such as conferences, sports events, cultural events, expos, and other events, Deaf people develop and maintain strong bonds with this second family of friends and associates.

In this chapter we'll help you develop some basic tools that will enable you to have effective and enjoyable communication about family life with your Deaf friends. After you finish this chapter, you will be able to use ASL to:

1. **Participate in a conversation to learn all about a Deaf person's family.**

2. **Demonstrate how two signs can be combined to form a new, compound sign.**

3. **Explain whether or not you get along with specific family members and why.**

4. **Describe family members in terms of qualities and personalities.**

5. **Describe family members in terms of age.**

6. **Share growing-up or "first-time" experiences with your Deaf friends.**

7. **Describe some of the educational and communicative options that hearing parents of Deaf children have to choose from.**

8. **Describe family members and their relationships in terms of Deaf and hearing communicative abilities.**

9. **Describe a Deaf person's second family and how this family evolved.**

10. **Communicate with your Deaf friends about family histories.**

11. **Demonstrate subordinate conjunctions through the technique of rhetorical "wh" questions.**

12. **Describe some possible differences between Deaf and hearing religious services.**

13. **Outline and tell in ASL, the Deaf-adapted fairy tale, "Fingerella."**

14. **Analyze and outline possible questions, comments, and behaviors to use with Deaf people and negative ones to avoid.**

15. **Describe the achievements of Deaf Arts Pioneer, Dr. Betty G. Miller.**

THE CLASSROOM

LEARNING ABOUT A DEAF PERSON'S FAMILY MEMBERS

Imagine you're at a Deaf gathering at Starbucks or some other Deaf event. You encounter new Deaf friends and you begin chatting with them. Maybe you are curious about their family backgrounds or maybe you have an assignment from your ASL instructor to explore Deaf friends' family relationships! What kind of questions would you use?

The next video is a typical dialogue between Bobby and Alice that will help you learn to do a chat about basic family information. This chat is similar to the one you saw in *My ASL Book, Level 1*. Watch the chat and write down the family information you learned from it.

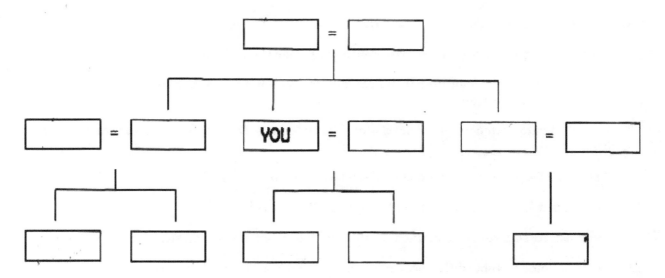

This is a tree of the family described in My ASL Tube 3-1. Use the information in the video to fill in the blanks in the family tree.

MY ASL TUBE 3-1: CHATTING ABOUT A BASIC FAMILY

Did you enjoy the chat? Were you able to fill out the family tree with all the names from the chat? Here is the English version of this conversation. You can use this as a model for chatting with Deaf people about their families:

ALICE: Hi!

BOBBY: Hello.

ALICE: Are you married?

BOBBY: Yes, I'm married.

ALICE: What's your wife's name?

BOBBY: My wife's name is Carla.

ALICE: Oh. Do you have children

BOBBY: Yes, I do.

ALICE: How many?

BOBBY: I have two children.

ALICE: What are their names?

BOBBY: They are Debbie and Ethan.

ALICE: Do you have brothers and sisters?

BOBBY: Yes, I do.

ALICE: How many?

BOBBY: I have an older brother and a younger sister. I'm in the middle.

ALICE: What are their names?

BOBBY: My brother's name is Harry and my sister's name is Jeannette.

ALICE: Is your brother or sister married?

BOBBY: Yes, they're both married.

ALICE: What's your brother's wife's name?

BOBBY: His wife's name is Karen.

ALICE: What's your sister's husband's name?

BOBBY: Her husband's name is Lonny.

ALICE: Does your brother have children?

BOBBY: Yes, he has a daughter and son.

ALICE: What're your brother's children's names?

BOBBY: Their names are Mark and Nancy.

ALICE: Does your sister have children?

BOBBY: Yes, she has a daughter.

ALICE: What's your sister's daughter's name?

BOBBY: Her name is Olivia.

ALICE: Are your parents still living?

BOBBY: Yes.

ALICE: What are your parents' names?

BOBBY: My Dad's name is Peter and my Mom's name is Rachel.

Here are the signs for a basic extended family that you learned in *My ASL Book, Level 1*.

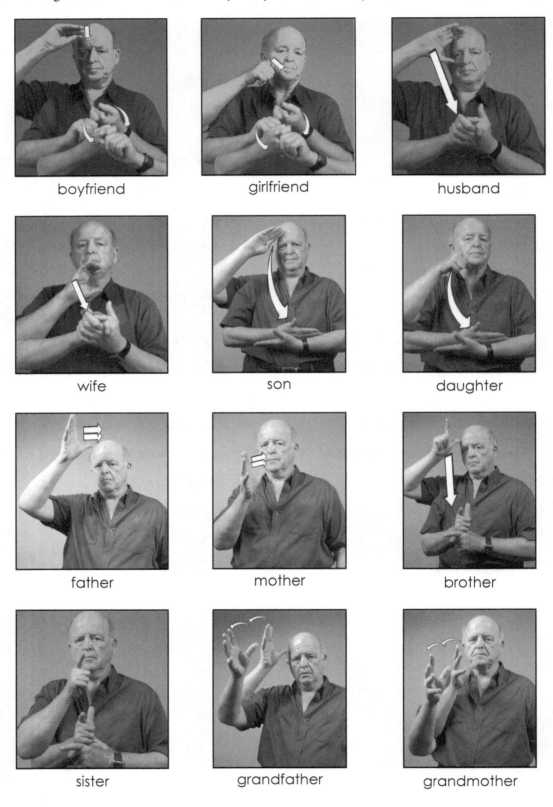

boyfriend

girlfriend

husband

wife

son

daughter

father

mother

brother

sister

grandfather

grandmother

grandson granddaughter uncle

aunt nephew niece

cousin in-law family

Let's review all the signs for a more complex family structure by re-visiting the love story from Chapter 4 of *My ASL Book, Level 1.*

MY ASL TUBE 3-2: GALLAUDET COLLEGE LOVE STORY, PART 2

I hope you remembered all the signs and that you can use these signs to chat with a Deaf friend about each other's family. Here are some of the signs you can use:

have an affair

find out

got mad

threw the bum out

separated

court

divorced

remarried

step- (relative)

half- (sibling)

drinking alcohol

rehab

sober

foster (parent/son/daughter/etc.)

lesbian

gay

straight

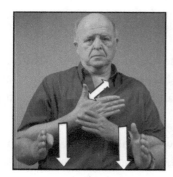

partner

adopted

old

died

dead

still living

house

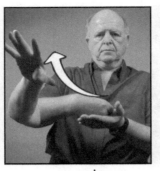
expensive

roommate

Now you have all the ASL tools you need for chatting with a friend about each other's families, warts and all. You can even use the information in your chat to build a family tree. Watch MY ASL TUBE and see how this can be done.

MY ASL TUBE 3-3: USING A CHAT TO BUILD A FAMILY TREE

Let's play the game in MY ASL TUBE 3-3 with a partner. First, chat with your partner about his/her family. As you interview your partner, develop a family tree based on what you learned. When you are finished, ask your partner to check the tree and make sure it is correct. Then, switch roles and have your partner interview you and create your family tree.

One caution: your family tree may be too small or only have one or two levels. Go ahead and lie! Make up additional family members and add them to your tree to make it a fuller tree complete with grandparents, grandchildren, etc. Ahem … my sister is Oprah Winfrey and my brother is Tom Cruise!

On the other hand, your family may be too big to chat about in a reasonable time period. My grandmother had 17 brothers and sisters, but that would be too large for creating a family tree. Instead, select four or five of your favorite brothers and sisters, aunts and uncles, cousins, etc., and use these relatives when you chat about a family tree.

Go ahead and have fun with this challenging exercise. The space below is blank for you and your partner to use to create a family tree. Be sure to use a pencil in case you need to erase your possible mistakes.

LINGUISTIC ILLUMINATIONS

COMPOUND SIGNS

When you chat with your Deaf friends about various family members, you'll find you sometimes need to combine two signs to create a sign for a new concept. For example, you can combine the signs for "mother" and "father" to create the sign for "parents." It makes the conversation flow more easily by using one sign for two people.

However, this poses a problem. As we learned in Chapter 5 of *My ASL Book, Level 1,* most nouns have two movements. So, if the sign for "father" has two movements and the sign for "mother" also has two movements, how can we combine them into the sign for "parents" but still have just two movements? After all, elementary math says 2 movements + 2 movements = 4 movements. What should you do?

To answer that question, we need to learn how to describe signs in terms of "movements" and "holds." These can be indicated by "M" and "H." For example, to make the sign for "mother" you MOVE your "5" hand to your chin, HOLD it there briefly, then MOVE it out and in and then HOLD it to the chin again. So, "mother" is represented by MOVEMENT-HOLD-MOVEMENT-HOLD or M-H-M-H. Similarly, "father" can be represented by M-H-M-H but at the forehead.

If we simply combined the two signs, we would have a cumbersome sign with four movements:

Mother + Father   → **Parents**

M-H-M-H + M-H-M-H   → M-H-M-H-M-H-M-H

But, during ASL's nearly 200-year history, as Deaf people adapted the French signs of Laurent Clerc and the native signs of Martha's Vineyard into a unique language, they developed a clever way to make sure that nouns kept their two-movement characteristics.

Draw your partner's family tree.

Watch MY ASL TUBE to see how they do this.

MY ASL TUBE 3-4: "MOTHER" AND "FATHER" COMPOUNDING INTO "PARENTS"

Did you see what happened? Instead of laboriously producing the signs for "mother" and "father" they created a new sign for "parents" by eliminating parts of the two original signs. This cutting out parts of two signs and combining the reduced signs into a new sign is a compounding process that is unique to signed languages the world over.

If we use MOVEMENT - HOLD notation, we can show how this compounding process works:

    Mother + Father   → **Parents**

(M-H-M-H) + (M-H-M-H)   → (M-H)-(M-H)

As you can see, one movement-hold has been eliminated from each original sign when they are used to form a compound sign. This satisfies the requirement of two movements for a noun.

Many other family signs also undergo this unique process of compounding. Watch MY ASL TUBE to learn some other examples of compounding for family signs.

MY ASL TUBE 3-5: OTHER COMPOUND FAMILY SIGNS

Did you enjoy learning this clever trick for compounding signs? Let's practice using these signs in the family tree diagram below. As you can see, there are pairs of relatives that can be indicated by a compound sign. Watch the video and fill in the blanks in the family tree diagram on the next page.

MY ASL TUBE 3-6: USING A CHAT ABOUT PAIRS OF RELATIVES TO FILL IN A FAMILY TREE

In addition to family signs, many other signs have been created through the process of compounding. Watch MY ASL TUBE and you'll see examples:

MY ASL TUBE 3-7: MORE EXAMPLES OF COMPOUNDED SIGNS

Here are the signs you saw in MY ASL TUBE. Remember that when two signs are compounded into a new sign, parts of each original sign are eliminated. Also, sometimes the two compounded signs will influence each other and change the signs:

 + 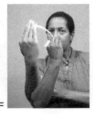 =   +  =

to eat   morning   breakfast   to eat   noon   lunch

Use the information from MAT 3-6 to fill in the blanks of this tree

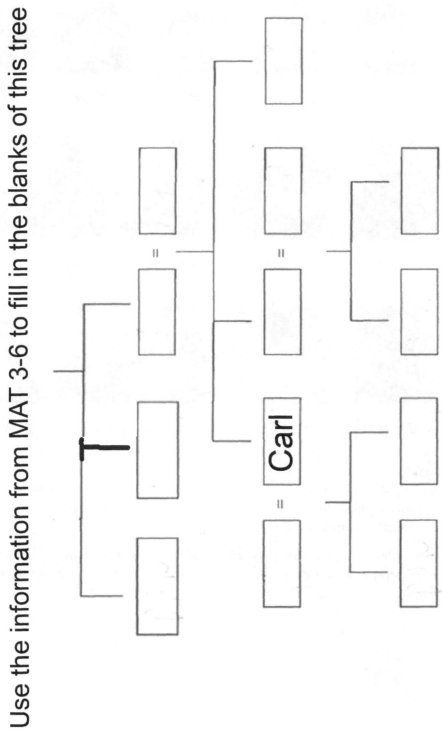

to eat   +   evening   =   dinner   money   +   to give   =   to buy

knowledge   +   to give out   =   to inform   knowledge   +   to stay   =   remember

to think   +   the same   =   to agree   to think   +   opposite   =   to disagree

When you were watching MY ASL TUBE, did you notice that, over time, the two signs in the compound influence each other until they blend into one fluid sign? This process is called assimilation; the individual signs assimilate with each other to produce a single sign.

Let's watch a video of "Raylene's Day." Raylene will tell you all about what happened to her one day. Watch the video and see if you can spot the compound signs. Write them all down in the chart on the next page.

Number	Sign meaning	Compounded from what two signs?	
1.			
2.			
3.			
4.			
5.			
6.			
7.			

MY ASL TUBE 3-8: Raylene's DAY

DEAF COFFEE NIGHT

GETTING ALONG WITH FAMILY MEMBERS

As you know, Deaf people are pretty direct and don't flinch from asking or answering questions about their own or their friends' family relationships. One thing they might ask is whether or not you get along with various family members. Here's how you might ask that question about a sister.

MY ASL TUBE 3-9: DO YOU GET ALONG WITH YOUR SISTER?

That's a pretty direct question, but Deaf people are not afraid to ask it. They would like to have a good picture of the dynamics of any family they may visit. It may be difficult for them to discover this information through interactions with family members. If these members do not know signs, your Deaf friends will feel obligated to let you know how well people in their families get along. On the other hand, hearing people might find it intrusive to be asked a question about how well they get along with certain relatives.

What do you think some of the responses to this question might be? Watch MY ASL TUBE and learn how a group of Deaf and hearing signers would respond to the question.

MY ASL TUBE 3-10: RESPONSES TO "HOW WELL DO YOU GET ALONG?"

Here are the responses, ranging from feeling close to not on speaking terms:

| close | pals/buddies | get along well | get along okay |

| don't get along | quarreling | getting into spats | not on speaking terms |

Now we'll play a game called the "hi!-erarchy totem pole game." A newly engaged Deaf couple, Bob and Janie, are chatting about their respective families and how well each of them gets along with various family members. Watch their conversation on MY ASL TUBE, and, based on their responses, construct two "Hi!-erarchy" totem poles. In other words determine how much they would like to say "Hi!" to each family member in the video. For example, if Bob is close to his grandmother, she goes at the top of Bob's totem pole since he likes to say "Hi!" and be in touch with her as often as possible. While, if Jane is not on speaking terms with her brother, he would be at the bottom of Jane's totem pole.

Use the diagram of the totem pole to add relatives.

MY ASL TUBE 3-11: BOB AND JANE'S FAMILY "TOTEM POLE GAME"

Did you get Bob and Jane's family totem poles correctly? Great! Now, work with a partner and create totem poles for you and your partner:

Your Family
Totem Pole

Partner's Family
Totem Pole

TALKING ABOUT VARIOUS QUALITIES AND PERSONALITIES OF FAMILY MEMBERS

If your Deaf friends tell you that they don't get along with certain relatives, you can just say "Oh!" and leave it at that. But, I suspect your curiosity will get the better of you and you'll want to know the reason why they get along or don't get along.

Consider yourself lucky to be a friend of Deaf people who follow Deaf cultural rules. After all, your hearing friends would probably never tell you that they didn't get along with certain relatives, much less why they didn't get along. But Deaf friends would probably be willing to share this information with you, assuming they trusted you.

Probably, the main reason people do or don't get along with certain relatives has to do with specific qualities of the relatives that affect their relationship. So, you need to know the signs for some of these qualities.

In the next MY ASL TUBE video, you'll see a Deaf person standing between two friends with opposite personal qualities. For example, one friend on the left is a snob while the other friend on the right is very friendly. The Deaf person will sign the personal quality of each friend and the friend will "act out" the quality. Try to guess what the sign means.

MY ASL TUBE 3-12: RELATIVES WITH OPPOSITE QUALITIES

Here are the qualities you learned from MY ASL TUBE:

| rich | poor | young | old |

| strong | weak | humble | famous | arrogant |

normal	weird	strange	friendly	snobbish
polite	rude		grouchy	sweet
ugly	cute	pretty	beautiful	handsome

Now that you've learned how to describe people's qualities, we're going to have some fun. Your Deaf friend Billie is going to take you to a family reunion where you'll meet all her relatives and family friends. Billee is Deaf and most of her relatives are hearing. None of them know how to sign, except a few basic gestures. So, Billee feels free to talk openly about each hearing family member or friend without worrying about whether she'll be "overheard." As you listen to Billee, please fill out the following table with the name of each family member or friend, his/her relationship to Billee, and his/her quality or characteristic. Have fun gossiping about Billee's family!

Family Member	Deaf or Hearing?	Name	Quality
1.			
2.			
3.			
4.			
5.			
6.			
7.			
8.			
9.			
10.			
11.			
12.			
13.			
14.			
15.			
16.			
17.			
18.			
19.			
20.			

MY ASL TUBE 3-13: FAMILY REUNION

CHATTING ABOUT FAMILY "GROWING-UP" EXPERIENCES

Once you've shared aspects of your Deaf friend's family members such as what's in the family tree, who gets along with who and which relative has what personal qualities, you'll want to go deeper. One way to do this is to share stories and experiences about growing up in your respective families. Deaf people love stories about their growing-up experiences, especially ones filled with humor and irony. So let's learn how to dig up and share these stories with one another.

First, though, you'll need to learn the signs for various ages. After all, if you want to understand a growing-up story, you need to know the storyteller's age when the growing-up event took place.

There are two types of signs for ages, the long form and the short form. The long form is more formal than the short form which is more casual. Watch MY ASL TUBE and learn the signs for each form. You should watch it several times to incorporate the nuances of the signs into your signing repertoire, especially the short form signs.

MY ASL TUBE 3-14: LONG AND SHORT FORM SIGNS FOR VARIOUS AGES

Now, let's imagine we're having a chat with a Deaf person about his family. You'll watch a video where the Deaf person will tell you the names and ages of all the relatives in her family. Use this information about the relative, whether he/she is Deaf or hearing, his/her name, and his/her age to fill out the chart below

Relative	Deaf or Hearing?	Name	Age
1.			
2.			
3.			
4.			
5.			
6.			
7.			
8.			
9.			
10.			
11.			
12.			
13.			
14.			
15.			

MY ASL TUBE 3-15: INFORMATION ABOUT FAMILY MEMBERS, INCLUDING AGES

How well did you do on this exercise? I hope you got all the correct information about the relatives. If you did, great! If not, go back and practice some more.

Now, we're going to learn to chat about various growing-up experiences by Deaf people. Sometimes the experiences happen where the storyteller was the only Deaf person in a hearing family or the only hearing CODA in a Deaf family. Other experiences involve a Deaf person in a Deaf family. We will look at four kinds of experiences:

1. Personal Development Events (e.g., learning to read, how to ask for a date, etc.)

2. Personal Discoveries (e.g., Santa is fake; where babies come from, etc.)

3. Family or School Celebrations (e.g., New Years, Valentine's Day, etc.)

4. Family Relationship Changes (e.g., birth of sibling; marriage, etc.)

Let's watch a video of two Deaf women who are sharing their life experiences. Each will give an age and name a "first-time" experience. Then they will "expand" on the life experience and provide interesting details. Write the type of event, the age it happened, the name of the event, and the expansion details. Write everything in the chart below.

Type of Event	Age	Event	Expansion Details
1.			
2.			
3.			
4.			
5.			
6.			
7.			
8.			
9.			
10.			
11.			
12.			
13.			
14.			
15.			
16.			

MY ASL TUBE 3-16: GROWING-UP EXPERIENCES

I'll bet all these "first-time" experiences brought back many memories. We can use these memories to play a game called "First-time winners." Here's how to play the game. Your class will be divided into four teams. Each team will pick a recorder and then team members will take turns telling the recorder some of their "first-time" experiences. The team picks the youngest age of team members for each "first time." After a length of time set by your instructor, the teams will report back to the class and share their first-time events, round-robin style. The team with the youngest age for each event wins a point. The team with the most points at the end wins the game.

THE ASL CLUB

FAMILY COMMUNICATION ISSUES

We've been learning about a variety of aspects of family relationships such as how well the families get along with your Deaf friends; some of the qualities that your Deaf friends have observed in their relatives; some life events and at what age they happened; and many other aspects of family life.

Now, we'll focus on one of the most vital aspects of Deaf-hearing family relations: how well the hearing and Deaf family members communicate with one another. This situation is much more complex and has a huge influence on whether or not the Deaf person will become an integral and close-knit member of his or her hearing family. Ideally, the hearing family members would all learn ASL and communicate with the Deaf member smoothly and easily. This is a case in most families headed by Deaf parents as well as the small number of families where the parents take the initiative and learn ASL. But, in the vast majority of hearing families with one or more Deaf members, this wonderful ideal is a wish unfulfilled.

Hearing parents who discover their baby is deaf find themselves bombarded with advice by hearing professionals such as doctors, audiologists, social workers, child development specialists, and many others. Rarely do any of these professionals recommend that the hearing parents get in touch with Deaf individuals and organizations to obtain guidance about how to raise a Deaf child. Think about it. Hearing parents with a newly diagnosed Deaf baby are full of fears of the future. How will their Deaf child learn? How will they take care of the child's needs? Will their Deaf child be dependent on the parents for the rest of their lives? And many more fearful questions. Imagine how these fears would be alleviated if they bonded with a Deaf person or Deaf couple. Such a relationship should help to increase their confidence in raising a Deaf child.

There is a poignant story that illustrates how this can work. It took place at The Learning Center (TLC), a bilingual K–12 school for Deaf children in Framingham, Massachusetts. TLC encourages interaction between hearing parents of Deaf children and Deaf community members. TLC sponsors support group meetings for parents where they can discuss and resolve issues that concern them about raising Deaf children. At one of these meetings, Marie Philip, the Deaf bilingual coordinator at TLC happened to mention that she would be flying to Vancouver, Canada, for a meeting. One of the hearing parents became very interested in Marie's plans. We can paraphrase the conversation that took place. We'll call the hearing mother Deborah:

Marie: I can't be with the support group next week because I'm flying to Vancouver, Canada for a conference.

Deborah: Vancouver, Canada. Wow, that's far. Will someone go with you to help you?

Marie: Why would I need someone to help me?

Deborah: You mean you'll be traveling alone?

Marie: Sure! I've done that many times.

Deborah: And there's never been any problems?

Marie: No. everything is fine.

Deborah: But you're Deaf. How do you communicate?

Marie: I use writing or gesture.

Marie saw the mother visibly relax and her face took on a relieved expression. Marie could almost read the thoughts racing through the mother's mind: "Everything will be alright. My son is Deaf but he will be fine."

As you can see, access to Deaf role models can provide a positive impact on hearing family members. Unfortunately, this kind of access is rare. Instead, many hearing professionals try to impose their agendas on the families, agendas that often deprive Deaf children from gaining a natural language and culture. Often, these professionals may insist that parents follow THEIR approach, no matter what.

You can imagine the confusion of many hearing families who discover one of their children is Deaf. One such family is the Tranchin family from Houston, Texas, who discovered that their four-year-old boy, Tommy, was Deaf. The father, Rob, a professional TV producer produced a video to chronicle the struggles that the family went through in search of a way to support their Deaf son. You'll need to search through YouTube to find the video titled "For a Deaf Son." The most recent YouTube URL is: https://www.youtube.com/watch?v=SCzl4kuWLw0. This is a very touching film so bring Kleenex. As you watch, you'll learn about how the Tranchins were bombarded with many approaches by various educators and professionals. No wonder hearing families are so confused.

As you can see from the video, the Tranchins ultimately decided on a bilingual approach, after many months of exploring and agonizing. Along the way, they learned about several other approaches. Can you describe these approaches?

Oral Approach: _____

_____

_____

_____

Total Communication: _____

_____

_____

_____

Cued Speech: _____

_____

_____

_____

Bilingual Approach: _____

_____

_____

_____

What does all this mean for your Deaf friends and their families? You'll find each Deaf person has to use a variety of strategies to communicate with hearing family members and friends, based on their communicative skills. They'll share with you how they deal with these varying levels of ASL skills. So you'll need to learn signs that can show various ASL skill levels

We'll show a continuum of skill levels in ASL that hearing family members might have achieved. We'll start with a person with zero ASL skills and progress up to an extremely fluent signer. Watch and learn:

MY ASL TUBE 3-17: LEVELS OF SIGN LANGUAGE FLUENCY

Here is the continuum you learned about. Most of these signs are unique to ASL and don't have an accurate English translation:

Naturally, the level of fluency of a Deaf person's family member will have an impact on whether or not that Deaf person wants to spend time with that family member. If the hearing family member does not know any signs, the Deaf person will be forced to use gestures or speech and lip-reading or notes written back-and-forth. Have you ever communicated by any of these methods? It can be a frustrating, slow, and tedious process. Additionally, in the case of speech and lip-reading, the Deaf person often has to do all the work of communicating. The hearing relative just has to speak slower while the Deaf person has to continually guess at what the relative is saying.

It's not much of an improvement if the hearing family member knows some signs but can barely communicate on a functional level. Some Deaf would prefer writing back-and-forth instead of communicating in sign language because the signs can be painfully slow eyesores. This creates a kind of catch-22—the hearing family members need frequent contact with their Deaf family member to improve their signing skills, but, if these signing skills are poor to begin with, the Deaf family members will probably minimize their time with these family members. Hopefully, the family will reach an ASL turning point and begin communicating in ways that are more comfortable for everyone.

A Deaf family member's desire to spend time with a hearing family member is proportional to the hearing family member's communicative skills. Let's practice this concept using a continuum form. In the next MY ASL TUBE, you'll see a Deaf woman talking about the skills of her hearing family members. She will identify the hearing family member and then describe that member's ASL skills. On the continuum form below, write the name of the hearing family member on the continuum line based on how much time you think the Deaf family member would want to spend with the hearing family member.

MY ASL TUBE 3-18: HOW MUCH TIME WOULD A DEAF PERSON SPEND WITH THIS RELATIVE?

Now you have a lot more skills in learning about your Deaf friends' relationships with their hearing family members, based on the personal qualities of the hearing family member and how well your Deaf friends get along and communicate with that hearing family member.

DEAF PEOPLE'S SOCIAL FAMILIES

In Chapter 1, we learned all the ways that Deaf people come together and celebrate their lives and the lives of other Deaf and hearing people. We also learned that Deaf people have two families, a biological family of mostly hearing people, and a social family of Deaf and hearing friends. Obviously, Deaf people don't have much choice in the biological families they are born into. But they acquire social families mostly by making choices among the people they meet. These people become part of their social family. Here are some examples of meetings that create bonds.

1. Fellow classmates and alumni of Deaf residential or mainstream schools.

2. Fellow Deaf or hearing sign-skilled students at college and universities.

3. Fellow athletes and fans of Deaf sports tournaments.

4. Fellow members of Deaf National, State, or regional organizations.

5. Participants in various Deaf club get-togethers.

6. New people at Deaf gatherings and events.

7. Fellow participants in Deaf church activities.

   And many more

Of course, just meeting another Deaf or hearing person at these events is no guarantee that he or she will become part of a Deaf person's family. Additional factors often come into play.

As one factor, the members of the Deaf person's social family usually have similar sign language styles. For example, the Deaf person may be fluent in "pure" ASL; His or her other social family members will often have a similar style. Or, if they don't, they'll make every effort to adjust their styles to fit in. As another example, the Deaf friend may have attended an oral school and uses a sort of "oralese" which is a mix of speech and signing. Members of this friend's social family may have this type of communication style. The need for similar communication styles is not a hard and fast rule; many Deaf people have friends with different styles, but, for the most part, similar styles rule.

Another factor will be shared experiences—the more the merrier. Perhaps the members of a Deaf person's social family all attended a residential school for the Deaf or perhaps they are all from a mainstreamed program. Perhaps everyone grew up in a family of hearing people and all have experienced being left out or facing communication problems. Or they all had Deaf parents or hearing parents who signed. Perhaps they attended the same college or university and had a similar educational experience. Having shared experiences helps make bonding and interactions flow much smoother. Everyone has the same basic experience so it is possible to go deeper, rather than needing to explain an experience to someone who has not had that kind of experience. There is wide variation in how much experiences count toward membership in a particular Deaf social family.

As another quality, members of a Deaf person's social family will often share similar values and beliefs. Perhaps they first met in some common ground and their values and beliefs will mirror that ground. For example, many of the clubs and organizations where they met have members with similar interests. Finally, even if there is a difference in values and beliefs, the social family will want to promote harmony and will either suppress their differences or "agree to disagree" but still maintain congenial relationships.

Let's go to MY ASL TUBE and meet some Deaf people who will tell you about a member of their social family. As you watch their stories, take note of their family members' names, how their relationship began, and what they have in common. Use this information to fill the chart below.

1. Family Member's name:	Deaf/Hearing?
How did relation start?	
What do they have in common?	
2. Family Member's name:	Deaf/Hearing?
How did relation start?	
What do they have in common?	
3. Family Member's name:	Deaf/Hearing?
How did relation start?	
What do they have in common?	
4. Family Member's name:	Deaf/Hearing?
How did relation start?	
What do they have in common?	
5. Family Member's name:	Deaf/Hearing?
How did relation start?	
What do they have in common?	
6. Family Member's name:	Deaf/Hearing?
How did relation start?	
What do they have in common?	
7. Family Member's name:	Deaf/Hearing?
How did relation start?	
What do they have in common?	

MY ASL TUBE 3-19: CHATTING ABOUT DEAF PEOPLE'S SOCIAL FAMILY

DEAF LIFE STORIES

We've learned so much about Deaf people's biological and social families! Now it is time to put it all together. We'll do this by watching some Deaf "life stories." During your interactions with Deaf people, you may have become close to a Deaf friend and gained enough trust that he or she is willing to "spill it all" in a story of his or her life from birth to the present. Consider this life story a wonderful gift from your Deaf friends and encourage them to tell the story.

To give you practice in learning about and understanding Deaf life stories, we'll show you four stories on MY ASL TUBE and invite you to write down details of each story in a questionnaire form. That way you can check to make sure that the details you thought you understood were the actual details. Good luck. Below is the questionnaire:

_____'s Story

1. When and how did the family discover that this family member was Deaf?

   _____

   _____

2. How did the family react and adjust to having a Deaf family member?

   _____

   _____

3. What kind of schooling did the family choose and how did the Deaf person cope?

   _____

   _____

4. What kind of sign language styles did the family develop from past to present?

   _____

   _____

5. How did the family's attitudes toward Deaf people and Deaf culture change over time?

   _____

   _____

_____'s Story

1. When and how did the family discover that this family member was Deaf?

   _____

   _____

2. How did the family react and adjust to having a Deaf family member?

   _____

   _____

3. What kind of schooling did the family choose and how did the Deaf person cope?

   _____

   _____

4. What kind of sign language styles did the family develop from past to present?

   _____

   _____

5. How did the family's attitudes toward Deaf people and Deaf culture change over time?

   _____

   _____

_____'s Story

1. When and how did the family discover that this family member was Deaf?

   _____

   _____

2. How did the family react and adjust to having a Deaf family member?

_____

_____

3. What kind of schooling did the family choose and how did the Deaf person cope?

_____

_____

4. What kind of sign language styles did the family develop from past to present?

_____

_____

5. How did the family's attitudes toward Deaf people and Deaf culture change over time?

_____

_____

_____'s Story

1. When and how did the family discover that this family member was Deaf?

_____

_____

2. How did the family react and adjust to having a Deaf family member?

_____

_____

3. What kind of schooling did the family choose and how did the Deaf person cope?

_____

_____

4. What kind of sign language styles did the family develop from past to present?

_____

_____

5. How did the family's attitudes toward Deaf people and Deaf culture change over time?

_____

_____

MY ASL TUBE 3-20: DEAF LIFE STORIES

ASL IN YOUR FACE

USING NMMS TO CREATE SUBORDINATING CONJUNCTIONS IN ASL

In Chapter 1, we learned about coordinating conjunctions. These are words that combine two independent sentences or clauses. For English, the most common conjunctions are "and," "but," "or," "so," and "yet." For ASL, the most common conjunctions are (in gloss): "wrong," "wrong-twist," "hit-finger," "happen," "finished," "find," "think-appear," "surprised," "frustrated."

English and ASL also have subordinating conjunctions. These words join an independent clause and a dependent clause. Here are examples (*the dependent clause is underlined and in italics*):

He didn't go to the beach *because it was raining*. OR
Because it was raining, He didn't go to the beach.

You can have dessert *as soon as you finish your vegetables*. OR
As soon as you finish your vegetables, you can have dessert.

By driving all day and all night, he made it to Phoenix by 7 a.m. OR
He made it to Phoenix by 7 a.m. *by driving all day and all night*.

Like English, ASL has many different techniques used to create subordinating conjunctions. In this chapter, we'll focus on one technique called a "rhetorical 'Wh' question." Using this technique, the signer creates a question and then answers the question. The result is a statement with two parts joined by the "rhetorical Wh" word. Let's look at an example:

Question: *He didn't go to the beach. Why?* **Answer:** *It was raining.*

Rhetorical "Wh" conjunction: He *didn't go to the beach. Why? It was raining.*

Why do we need rhetorical questions? Mainly to show a causal relationship between two events or facts. We make the caused event or fact into a question and then show what caused the event by adding a rhetorical "Wh" and an answer. In the previous example, the caused event was "He didn't go to the beach" and the event that caused this was "It was raining."

Now we'll show you the three subordinating conjunctions from the previous page and how you can convert them to a rhetorical "Wh" question form.

MY ASL TUBE 3-21: CREATING STATEMENTS USING RHETORICAL WH QUESTIONS

Did you notice that the rhetorical "Wh" has a different NMM than a "Wh" question? Watch the next MY ASL TUBE to see the difference.

MY ASL TUBE 3-22: NMMS FOR "WH" QUESTIONS AND RHETORICAL "WH" QUESTIONS

Here's what you learned from MAT 3-21:

Eyebrows furrowed →

Head thrust forward →

Eyebrows raised →

Head tilted upward →

Wh Question NMM   Rhetorical Wh Question NMM

What "Wh" words can you use for a rhetorical question sentence? Almost all of them! Here are ten of the most popular "wh" words to use:

who?   what?   when?   where?   why?

how?   what for?   how much?   what happened?   from where?

Let's practice. On MY ASL TUBE, you'll see some signed sentences. Break each sentence into resulting event, "wh" word, and cause of resulting event. The first one has been done for you.

Resulting Event	"Wh" word	Cause of resulting event
1. She bought a pizza	Why?	Friend visited her home
2.		
3.		
4.		
5.		
6.		
7.		
8.		
9.		
10.		
11.		
12.		

MY ASL TUBE 3-23: MORE EXAMPLES OF RHETORICAL "WH" QUESTION SENTENCES

A word to the wise. You may find the rhetorical question fascinating and want to use it as much as possible. DON'T. You can use the rhetorical question as a way to emphasize a causal relationship, but do it sparingly. Sometimes hearing sign language students (and Deaf people themselves) go overboard and use rhetorical questions for almost every sentence. The result can be hilarious. Watch the next MY ASL TUBE and you'll understand why.

MY ASL TUBE 3-24: RHETORICAL QUESTION OVERLOAD!

ASK MISS ASLEY: THE DEAFINITE ANSWER

(Miss ASLey is a Deaf professional etiquettarian. In other words, she feels it is her duty to remind various uninformed people whenever they make a cultural faux pas and to show them the proper cultural behavior to exhibit toward people in the Deaf world. If you want to learn how to show proper humility toward Deaf people, Miss ASLey is the person you need to ask.)

Dear Miss ASLey,

I have a Deaf son, Jonathan, who just became three years old. When Jonathan was a baby, the hospital put him through infant screening and found that he was profoundly deaf. I decided to sign up for ASL classes, so I could communicate with my son. My doctor and an audiologist both advised against it, but I went ahead anyway. That's because I have a Deaf cousin who is an architect. His Deaf wife is a high school math teacher. They both use ASL and they told me that language really helped them succeed in life. They said that what deaf children needed most of all was to learn a first language, ASL, instead of suffering through speech and lip-reading training and learning almost nothing. Their ideas really influenced me to take ASL classes. I also decided to take my son to Deaf community events to help him become more aware of his future "second family."

Here's the problem, Miss ASLey. Every time I go to an event, Deaf people will offer unsolicited advice about how to raise my son. The first thing they always ask is not "Hold old is he?" But "Is he Deaf or hearing?" Once they find out he's Deaf, they offer me lots of advice about how to communicate with a Deaf child, how to raise him, what school to send him to, and on and on. Several of them suggested that I send Jonathan away to the state school for the deaf which is five hours from our home rather than to the local school which has mainstreamed classes. Miss ASLey, I respect their excitement about a new Deaf person, but I feel that a lot of their advice is an invasion of our privacy. I'd prefer that they not offer so much advice without my asking them. But I don't want to hurt their feelings by telling them to back off, especially since Jonathan may someday need to be a part of their community.

What should I do? How can I find a good solution for myself, Jonathan, and the Deaf people that we meet at Deaf community events?

Signs of Perplexity,

Amanda

***

Dear Amanda,

First of all, Miss ASLey commends you on the excellent choices you've made for your Deaf son. You have done this despite the efforts of many doctors, audiologists, speech pathologists, and other so-called professionals to push a short-sighted and narrow agenda that does not include ASL and Deaf culture. They do so out of a mistaken belief that if Deaf children learn ASL, it will interfere with their development of speech and language skills. My dear Amanda, during my college days (probably before you were born), I took a two-year course in French and when I finished, my English language skills were exactly the same, if not better. So, if my French studies did not interfere with my English language skills, do you think that Jonathan's acquisition of ASL will interfere with his English language skills? Of course not! I don't generally wear a hat, but, if I did, I would doff it to you in honor of your wise choices for your son.

As for the unsolicited advice by Deaf community people, wouldn't you agree that their advice is above and beyond the atrocious advice that the hearing so-called professionals have been giving you? In fact, this advice is the product of personal experiences of Deaf people which have been shared and analyzed among themselves and with hearing friends and family members. Every one of those solicitous Deaf individuals loves your son to death because he will someday take his place in their community (as you will, too). So, before you become concerned about your "privacy," consider where all this advice is coming from and be grateful that you have a huge family of Deaf people to offer help in raising your Deaf son. That is gold!

Of course there is the practical problem of wading through a huge volume of Deaf community advice about raising your son. Perhaps the best approach is simply to say "Thank you for your advice. I'll think about it." to anyone who offers suggestions about raising Jonathan. This response is a polite way of saying you respect the Deaf person's ideas but you are the one who ultimately makes the decision about Jonathan's upbringing. Even if you don't follow the advice, at least you did consider it.

If you thirst for more information and ideas, you may want to google "American Society for Deaf Children," an organization that brings Deaf adults and hearing parents together to optimize opportunities for Deaf children. They can help you to continue to make wise decisions about your son's upbringing.

Miss ASLey wishes you the very best success in raising a fine young Deaf gentleman who will offer so much to the Deaf community.

Advisedly yours,

Miss ASLey

FINGER-SPELLING FINESSE

SOME FINGER-SPELLING GAMES

You can increase your skill in finger-spelling various words by playing various games:

SPELL THAT CATEGORY: It's a fairly simple game. Your instructor or club leader can divide up your ASL class into teams of four or five players. Each team picks a recorder who writes down the words that team members finger-spell to him/her in turn. The instructor gives all the teams a category and play begins. After a certain time limit, the game stops and each team compares the number of finger-spelled words on their list. The team with the most finger-spelled words wins the game. Here are some possible categories you can use in the game:

1. Farm animals
2. Zoo animals
3. Car brands
4. Diseases
5. Fruits and vegetables
6. Furniture
7. States
8. State capitals
9. Major cities
10. School subjects
11. Articles of clothing
12. TV shows
13. Movie titles
14. Candy brands
15. Drinks

BEFORE AND AFTER: This is a variation of the above game. Players form small teams and pick a category. The first player finger-spells a word in that category and the second person then finger-spells another word in the category that starts with the last letter of the first person's word. For example: First person: GiraffE; Second person: ElephanT; Third person: TigeR; and so on. If a team member can't think of a word, the team is awarded 1 "loser" point and the next person picks a new word. The team with the least "loser" points wins the game.

EXTENDED FINGER-SPELLED STORY: A team or group tells a story in round-robin style. The first storyteller signs one sentence in the story and finger-spells a word. This is the cue for the second person to add the next sentence to the story and he/she in turn finger-spells a word. The words have to start with letters in alphabetical order. For example: First player: Once upon a time there was a girl named A-n-n-i-e; Second player: Annie liked to go B-o-w-l-i-n-g; Third player while Annie was bowling, her shoe was c-a-u-g-h-t; and so on.

These are all fun ways to improve your finger-spelling skills.

SIGNS FROM THE REAL WORLD

Deaf people love to take fairy tales or stories and create their own Deaf versions. For example, several theater productions have mounted adaptations of *Romeo and Juliet* in which Romeo is hearing from a hearing family and Juliet is Deaf from a Deaf family or vice-versa. These productions showed the challenges that face Deaf-hearing married couples and their families and how they could be overcome (or not).

We're going to show you an entertaining children's fairy tale that has been adapted to reflect Deaf viewpoints and values. The title of the story is "Fingerella." If it sounds familiar, it is!!

Watch, enjoy, and absorb the story, then answer the questions below.

MY ASL TUBE 3-25: FINGERELLA

1. How did Ella's Deaf parents make a living in the old days?

_____

_____

2. After her Deaf parents died, how did Ella get along with her stepmother and stepsisters? What name did they give her?

_____

_____

3. How was the attitude of the King and Queen toward their Deaf son different from the stepmother and stepsisters' attitude toward Fingerella?

_____

_____

4. How did Fingerella survive the cruel treatment of her stepmother and stepsisters?

_____

_____

5. How different was the Deaf Prince's reaction to the stepsisters compared to his reaction to Fingerella?

_____

_____

6. After Fingerella ran away at the stroke of midnight, how did the Deaf Prince succeed in finding her?

_____

_____

DEAF MYTHBUSTERS

By now, you, the student have become much more sensitive about what kind of questions or comments you can make with your Deaf friends. As a knowledgeable ASL student, you know for sure that the following questions or comments are definite no-noes:

1. **Is sign language universal?**

2. **Can you drive a car?**

3. **Are you hearing-impaired?**

4. **Wow! You speak very well for a Deaf person!**

5. **Any other question or comment that brings up false information or suggests that Deaf people can't do some things that hearing people can.**

There are other topics that need to be approached carefully. For sure, these topics should only be broached after you get to know a new Deaf friend very well. Otherwise, you'll come off looking like a scientist doing research on human subjects rather than a person who wants to develop a deeper relationship with his/her Deaf friends. Be prepared to hear strong opinions about these topics:

1. **What do you think of cochlear implants? (or any other audio device)**

2. **How do you feel about musical activities like dancing, singing songs, or listening to or playing musical instruments?**

3. **Are you part of the disabled people's club or organization?**

4. **Do you know my Deaf friend Bob? (if he is local, okay, if he lives a thousand miles away, probably not okay)**

Finally, there are positive topics which Deaf people will enjoy chatting about such as:

1. What do you think of Deaf Gain?

2. Where can I go to meet Deaf people?

3. What are the most positive activities in our community?

Additionally, there are behaviors that you should never do even if you have limited ASL skills:

1. Talking loudly so they can hear you better or speaking very slowly so they can lip-read you better. Your Deaf friends will feel as if you think they're morons.

2. Getting a Deaf person's attention by throwing something at them, even if it is a pillow or a marshmallow.

3. Staring like an idiot at Deaf people having a conversation that you are not part of.

4. Chewing gum while conversing with Deaf friends. Since your friend has to watch you sign, he or she is going to feel like a farmer watching a cow chewing her cud.

5. If the Deaf person is relying on an interpreter for communication, acting like he or she is a third party. Instead of saying "Tell him, I said ...," just speak directly to the Deaf person and let the interpreter facilitate your conversation.

6. Wearing bright flashy jewelry, long, over-decorated fingernails, clothing with busy patterns, or anything else that distracts from being able to read signs.

It would be a great idea for your class to have a discussion about positive comments and behaviors to use with Deaf people and negative ones to avoid. Your ASL instructor can give you lots of good information about this.

DEAF CULTURE CORNER: HEROES AND SHE-ROES

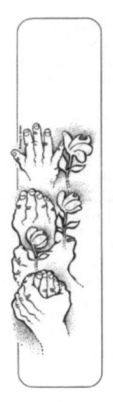

Betty G. Miller

Photographer: Cuppa Jo. Coyright Purple Swirl Arts

DR. BETTY G. MILLER, DEAF ARTS PIONEER EXTRAORDINAIRE

This multi-talented Deaf woman was a pioneer in so many performing and visual artistic endeavors that it would take a long time to describe them all. But we will try!

Betty was born in the Chicago area to Deaf parents in 1934. Her father, Ralph R. Miller, Sr. was an accomplished professional illustrator. Betty had two older hearing brothers and her parents assumed that she was also hearing. However, when she reached kindergarten age, it was discovered that she was hard of hearing and her Deaf parents felt that she would be better off attending an oral school and later a school for hearing students. So, instead of being enrolled in her father's Alma Mater, the Illinois School for the Deaf where sign language was the mode of instruction, Betty was enrolled in the Bell School, an oral program where signs were not permitted. She later was transferred to a regular school for hearing children. Throughout her childhood, she endured many hours of speech training. Betty grew up in two worlds, her hearing school world where she strained to communicate through speech and lip-reading, and the Deaf world of her parents and their friends, where she used ASL with ease. Her experiences in an oral world were the subject of some controversial art, many years later.

After high school, she enrolled in Southern Illinois University, but there were no support services for Deaf or hard-of-hearing students. After an exhausting year of struggling to survive as the sole hard-of-hearing person in a sea of hearing students, she transferred to Gallaudet College, then, and still, the only college/university program for Deaf people.

At Gallaudet, she experienced a huge culture shock as she encountered Deaf college classmates, most of whom were fluent signers. American Sign Language had been the language of her parents' older generation, so it was a shock to encounter people of her own age who used sign language. But, during her four years at Gallaudet, she left behind her struggle as a hard-of-hearing person in a hearing environment and embraced the Gallaudet experience. When she graduated in 1957, she clearly identified herself with a different struggle, the acceptance and support of Deaf culture and sign language even before it had been identified as a legitimate language.

After graduation from Gallaudet, Betty followed in her father's footsteps and became a commercial artist. However, she still felt drawn to a different artistic life and she became a faculty member in the Department of Art at Gallaudet. There, she taught and mentored many art students who used art in a variety of careers and settings. She also set about learning as much as she could and was successful in securing a doctorate from University of Pennsylvania, the first Deaf female Gallaudet graduate to achieve this milestone.

Betty's love of the newly declared American Sign Language led her to a second career in the performing arts. She was involved in the Drama Guild of the District of Columbia Club of the Deaf (DCCD) in roles such as actor, director, scenic designer, and other roles. In 1966, Betty and her colleagues decided to launch a new drama organization which was independent from DCCD. The name of the new group was the Frederick Hughes Memorial Theater, named in honor of a popular Deaf theater instructor at Gallaudet who died on the stage at Gallaudet after accepting a yearbook dedication during Betty's junior year.

Hughes Memorial Theater went on to blaze many new trails in Deaf theater arts. One of its most memorable productions was "Dark of the Moon," a folk drama with music performed by a cast of Deaf and hearing performers. Betty directed the play and also designed a simple but rustic set as befitting mountain people. One of the scenes from this play, a wild revival scene, won the District of Columbia One-Act Play Tournament in 1968. The cast and crew then entered the national tournament and came within a hair's breadth of winning a national title.

Betty made another contribution when she designed the set for "We and They," a Deaf-awareness show presented at University of Maryland. The set was basically a set of large blocks which, when arranged one way, formed a wall with the motif "We and They," but when re-arranged, produced a different wall which showed a huge "I Love You (ILY)" sign. The ILY sign had first appeared in the early 1900s, but never gained wide usage. However, Betty's artwork re-inspired many people and, over time, the ILY sign became a frequent expression of goodwill among Deaf and hearing people.

As Betty became more and more aware of issues in Deaf culture and community, she began to experiment with art that would reflect these issues. One huge issue was the oral oppression in Deaf education. In many schools, Deaf primary students were often segregated and had to endure the same oral education that Betty had gone through many years before. So, she created a collection of fifteen paintings in oil and acrylics that reflected the oppression of Deaf people by their hearing educators and exhibited the collection at a faculty art show in 1972. As Deborah Sonnenstrahl described it in Deaf Artists in America, Miller's collection, "demonstrated her relationship to the world as a deaf child. She showed hands bound by chains, deaf children with puppet-like mouths, deaf children weighed down by their heavy hearing aids, children bound in a stockade … The works sent a strong message that deaf people were indeed oppressed."

People, both Deaf and hearing, reacted to the exhibition with shock and consternation. Many criticized the works as being too "negative." But, gradually, people began to recognize and accept the messages contained in her artwork and to acknowledge the oppression of Deaf students by hearing educators in schools for the Deaf everywhere. It took some time, but people began to explore and realize this issue in greater and greater depth.

In 1975, the World Federation of the Deaf held its Seventh Congress in Washington, D.C., with the theme of "Full Citizenship for All Deaf People," a theme that Betty's artwork strongly supported. At the Congress, Betty, Chuck Baird, and other Deaf artists met with a hearing arts professional named Janette Norman who advocated for the establishment of a Deaf Artists' Colony located somewhere in the U. S.

Events followed quickly and Spectrum, Focus on Deaf Artists (Spectrum, FODA), was established in Austin, Texas, with several goals, among them: 1) To serve as a clearinghouse and cultivate exchanges among Deaf artists in the U.S. and Internationally; 2) To document the history and preserve the works of Deaf artists; and 3) To establish a liaison and cultivate exchanges between the Deaf and hearing art worlds. Betty Miller was asked to assume a leadership role at Spectrum FODA. Betty was torn between her secure job as an art professor at Gallaudet and her need to foster new forms of arts that reflected Deaf people's experience.

In 1977, she finally decided to take the courageous step of resigning from her tenured position at Gallaudet and become a leader of this new arts organization. Janette Norman had been able to secure grants from Helen DeVitt Jones, a wealthy woman from an oil-baron family which paid administrative salaries and from a federal program called CETA that provided stipends to support the many Deaf artists who became part of the Spectrum family. Betty and her friend Clarence Russell Jr. bought a ranch just outside of Austin, Texas and it became the home of the new artists' colony.

Spectrum grew and blossomed with all sorts of projects in visual arts, dance, performing arts, film, video, writing, and many other areas of artistry. There were also summer camps for kids, Deaf arts programs for schools, and summer conferences attended by Deaf artists from all over the U. S. Spectrum was staffed mostly by Deaf artists who moved to Austin to join the company.

Over the next five years, Spectrum FODA created many successful programs and works of visual and performing arts. Alas, some good things do come to an end. Helen Jones encountered some financial issues and had to stop supporting Spectrum. The CETA program began to have problems as well. So, in 1980, Spectrum was closed down, despite its countless achievements.

Betty Miller continued to develop her artwork and to serve as a leader in the Deaf visual and performing arts world. She sponsored several salons and frequently consulted with a variety of artists. Betty also became the first Deaf certified addictions counselor and helped many Deaf alcoholics and substance abusers find their way on the road to recovery. Based on her experiences as a counselor, she wrote *Deaf & Sober: Journeys through Recovery*, a National Association of the Deaf publication.

Despite the loss of Spectrum, Betty still held the dream of Deaf arts in her heart and mind. In May 1989, just before the inauguration of the Deaf Way Arts Festival at Gallaudet University, Betty Miller and Paul Johnston led a four-day workshop of Deaf artists. Out of this workshop, they created a De'VIA (Deaf View/Image Art) Movement. Their manifesto can be found at the website www.deafart.org.

Dr. Betty Miller died on December 3, 2012, after a lifetime of contributions to the Deaf Art World. She was survived by her partner of twenty-five years, Nancy Creighton, who continues to promote Betty's goals and ideals. Later, The Betty G. Miller Fellowship Award was established in her honor by the International Alumnae of Delta Epsilon Sorority at Gallaudet University. This award provides financial assistance to Deaf women pursuing doctoral degrees.

You can see a beautiful biography in ASL of Dr. Betty Miller here:

MY ASL TUBE 3-26: DR. BETTY G. MILLER, DEAF ARTS PIONEER EXTRAORDINAIRE

HOW DID I DO?

I hope you enjoyed all the things you learned in this chapter. You can use your new skills and knowledge to interact comfortably with Deaf people about their biological and social families. It's a good idea to check your progress. Below are the goals for the chapter along with a continuum from "I did great!" to "I need to work on this more." Write an "x" in the place that you feel reflects your progress in this chapter.

Now that you have finished Chapter 3, you, the student, can use ASL to:

1. Participate in a conversation to learn all about a Deaf person's family.

    ←───→

    I need to work on this more   I did great!

2. Demonstrate how two signs can be combined to form a new, compound sign.

    ←───→

    I need to work on this more   I did great!

3. Explain whether or not you get along with specific family members and why.

    ←───→

    I need to work on this more   I did great!

4. Describe family members in terms of qualities and personalities.

    ←───→

    I need to work on this more   I did great!

5. Describe family members in terms of age.

    ←───→

    I need to work on this more   I did great!

6. Share growing-up or "first-time" experiences with your Deaf friends.

    ←───→

    I need to work on this more   I did great!

7. Describe some of the educational and communicative options that hearing parents of Deaf children have to choose from.

    ←───→

    I need to work on this more   I did great!

8. Describe family members and their relationships in terms of Deaf and hearing communicative abilities.

←──→

I need to work on this more   I did great!

9. Describe a Deaf person's second family and how this family evolved.

←──→

I need to work on this more   I did great!

10. Communicate with your Deaf friends about family histories.

←──→

I need to work on this more   I did great!

11. Demonstrate subordinate conjunctions through the technique of rhetorical "wh" questions.

←──→

I need to work on this more   I did great!

12. Describe some possible differences between Deaf and hearing religious services.

←──→

I need to work on this more   I did great!

13. Outline and tell in ASL, the Deaf-adapted fairy tale, "Fingerella."

←──→

I need to work on this more   I did great!

14. Analyze and outline possible questions, comments, and behaviors to use with Deaf people and negative ones to avoid.

←──→

I need to work on this more   I did great!

15. Describe the achievements of Deaf Arts Pioneer, Dr. Betty G. Miller.

←──→

I need to work on this more   I did great!

Life in the "Learning Box" of the Deaf World

CHAPTER 4

INTRODUCTION TO THE CHAPTER

Years ago, I read a book that had a powerful impact on my life. The book was titled "The Three Boxes of Life," and was written by Richard Bolles, who was also the author of the popular series "What Color is Your Parachute?" In his book, Mr. Bolles used the idea of "Three Boxes" to signify the three stages of life that most people go through: (1) Learning, (2) Working, and (3) Playing (leisure time activities). As children and youth, we are primarily involved in getting an education. As young adults, we join the working world and pursue a career. Finally, as retirees, we focus our lives primarily on leisure time activities. Bolles believed that people sell themselves short by segmenting their life stages into these three boxes of life. Instead, he felt it was possible to pursue all three activities—learning, working, and playing—throughout life.

In the next two chapters, we'll explore various aspects of the life processes of learning, working, and playing as it relates to Deaf people. In this way, we'll gain new ways of communicating with Deaf people and interacting with Deaf culture in a variety of situations.

After you complete Chapter 4, you'll be able to use ASL to:

1. **Describe the process of applying to and enrolling in a college or university.**

2. **Demonstrate correct usage of auxiliary verbs in ASL.**

3. **Outline some of the support services offered to Deaf and hard of hearing college and university students.**

4. **Identify some majors and minors, as well as courses and classes, and the process by which students complete their education.**

5. **Outline some of the staff and student positions at a college or university.**

6. **Describe personal qualities you find among members of the campus community.**

7. **Analyze some of the culture shock issues raised by the experiences of Dr. Madan Vasishta when he first became a student at Gallaudet University.**

8. **Summarize some typical mini-biographies of Deaf college or university students and compare them to your own autobiographies.**

9. **Discuss what it means to be a hearing or Deaf ally of Deaf college students.**

10. **Outline and give examples of some of the major categories of careers.**

11   Make excuses or give reasons for not meeting your school or work obligations.

12.   Outline the Life Story of Dr. Madan Vasishta, Deaf Indian Education Pioneer.

THE CLASSROOM

APPLYING TO AND ENROLLING IN A COLLEGE OR UNIVERSITY

If you are a high school, college, or university student, you are probably looking forward to a time when, with a sigh of relief, you can say, "no more pencils, no more books, no more teacher's dirty looks." But, the world is changing so fast that you will most likely need to participate in life-long learning to keep up with new ideas within your career, your family life, and your leisure time activities. Your employer may require you to take a training course before you can start a new job. Or, you may switch to a new career that requires new training. When you marry and begin a family, you'll need new skills for dealing with various family situations. When you make plans to travel the world, you may want to learn a foreign language so you can communicate with the people you meet. More down-to-earth concerns: If you get a ticket for a traffic violation, you'll probably try to get it dismissed by going to traffic school; if you've put on a little too much around the middle, there's a school for Zumba; If you like to cook, a cooking school beckons. The possibilities are endless. It's a good idea to learn how to communicate about learning with your Deaf friends and acquaintances, be they classmates, educational staff, or faculty.

Most of us think of the learning box as something that happens during the first twenty or so years of our lives. You thought your education was over the moment you walked across the stage and got your college diploma. But learning is a life-long process. Hopefully, you'll let go of the idea of a learning "box" and commit yourself to learning throughout life. After all, "thinking outside of the box" shouldn't just be an expression, but an integral element of people's lives.

You have already learned some signs for school learning experiences. Let's review them here:

Elementary school	*Middle school*	*Junior high school*
High school	*College*	*University*
Residential school	*Mainstreamed school*	*Gallaudet University*
National Technical Institute for the Deaf	*California State University, Northridge*	

Many of you are still in high school or college, so we'll learn how to communicate with Deaf people in ASL about the whole college experience. We'll follow your Deaf friends from the time they first thought about going to college until they graduated to the cheers and the tears of parents and grandparents, classmates and friends. We'll start by watching a video of Deaf people going through the application and enrollment process for a college or university of their choice.

MY ASL TUBE 4-1: APPLYING AND ENROLLING IN COLLEGE OR UNIVERSITY

Here are some of the signs you saw in MY ASL TUBE. These are typical of both Deaf and hearing college and university students:

applying   filling out a form   personal statement

entrance exams   interviewing   being accepted   not being accepted

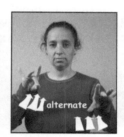

registering   counselor   picking classes   transferring

LINGUISTIC ILLUMINATIONS

USING AUXILIARY VERBS IN ASL FOR PERSONAL STATEMENTS AND INTERVIEWS

When Deaf college or university applicants write personal statements or respond to interview questions, they often need to be able to use auxiliary or "helping" verbs to clarify their situations. "Helping" verbs will enable them to share their achievements, their knowledge and skills that will enable them succeed in their chosen fields, and their goals for their college education and professional careers. That's where auxiliary verbs come into the picture.

You have already learned two auxiliary verbs and one adverb that help to establish the tense of whatever information Deaf people want to communicate. The verbs: are "finished," and "will" and the adverb is "since-to-now" Here are the signs for these three auxiliaries:

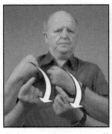

finished (past tense)   "since-to-now"   "will" (future)
                               (past perfect)

Below is a timeline that shows you how these three auxiliaries demonstrate tense:

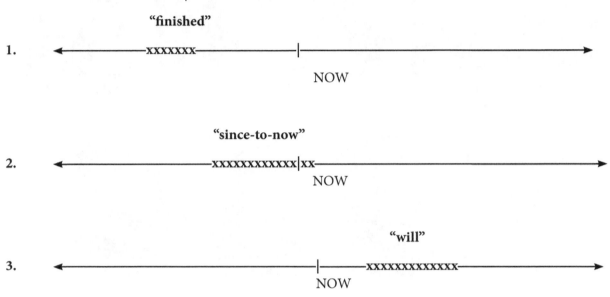

"finished"

1.   ◄────────────xxxxxxx─────────────┼──────────────────────►

                                    NOW

"since-to-now"

2.   ◄───────────xxxxxxxxxxxx|xx──────────────────────►

                                    NOW

"will"

3.   ◄────────────────────────┼───────xxxxxxxxxxxx──────────►

                                    NOW

In ASL, you can usually put tense auxiliaries such as "Finished," "Since-to-now" and "Will" in any one of three places. For example, you can place the auxiliary "will":

1.   At the beginning and end of the sentence. Example: ***Will*** she walk, ***will.***

2.   Between the subject and the verb" Example: She ***will*** walk.

3.   At the end of the sentence. Example: She walk, ***will.***

All three sentences are acceptable in ASL, but only one sentence is acceptable in English.

Which one is it? You're right, it's sentence # 2.

Let's watch MY ASL TUBE for some other auxiliary verbs.

MY ASL TUBE 4-2: NEGATIVE AUXILIARIES AND MODALS

Did you enjoy learning the new verbs? Let"s expand our understanding.

The two negative auxiliaries are "not" and "not-yet." These are used to negate "finished," "Since-to-now," and "will" auxiliaries. These two negatives can be used in the same places in sentences. For example:

NOT:

1. *Not* she learn ASL, **_not_**.

2. She **_not_** learn ASL

3. She learn ASL, **_not_**

NOT-YET

1. *Not-yet* she learn ASL, **_not-yet_**.

2. She **_not-yet_** learn ASL

3. She learn ASL, **_not-yet_**

Not   not-yet

Important: The two auxiliaries have different meanings. Look at these two examples:

1. *"Me married not"* means I am not married now and haven't made any plans to be so.

2. *"Me married not-yet"* means I am not married now but plan to get married in the future.

Another category of auxiliary verbs that you learned from MY ASL TUBE involves modals. These types of helping verbs are used to express ability, possibility, permission, or obligation. We will learn to use four positive modals and their negative or opposite modals. Here they are:

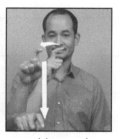

can, could   can't, couldn't   must   not have to

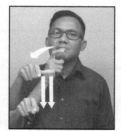
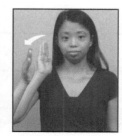
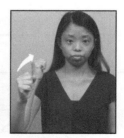

need to   not need to   will, would   won't wouldn't

In ASL, you can usually put any of these modals in the same positions as you can put the tense auxiliaries. In other words, you can put modals such as "can," "can't," "must," "not have to," "need to," "not need to," "will," "won't," and other modals in the following positions in any ASL sentence (we will use "can" in our examples):

1. At the beginning and end of the sentence. Example: **<u>Can</u>** she walk, **<u>can.</u>**

2. Between the subject and the verb. Example: She **<u>can</u>** walk.

3. At the end of the sentence. Example: She walk **<u>can.</u>**

Again, all three sentences are acceptable in ASL, but only the second is acceptable in English.

Now that we know how to use some tense auxiliaries and modals, let's watch a MY ASL TUBE video of Deaf college applicants expressing their personal statements or answering interview questions, using tense auxiliaries or modals. Use the information to fill in the following table:

#. Write the sentence in English	Auxiliary
1.	
2.	
3.	
4.	
5.	
6.	
7.	
8.	
9.	
10.	
11.	
12.	

MY ASL TUBE 4-3: PERSONAL AND INTERVIEW STATEMENTS USING AUXILIARIES

THE ASL CLUB

PROVIDING COMMUNICATION ACCESS FOR DEAF COLLEGE AND UNIVERSITY STUDENTS

There is one more step in the application process. Deaf college and university students have to go the extra mile to get an education. These students need support for communication access to their professors, to college staff members, to fellow students and to any other member of the campus community. In the next MY ASL TUBE video, we'll learn the signs for various college and university support services for Deaf students.

MY ASL TUBE 4-4: DEAF SUPPORT SERVICES

Here are the signs that you learned from MY ASL TUBE:

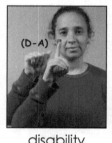

disability   support services   interpreter

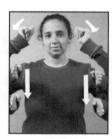

tutor   transcriptionist   video phone

Getting these services can be more challenging because the services must be scheduled in advance. For regularly scheduled classes, the services can be booked at the beginning of the semester and remain consistent throughout. However, for unscheduled events such as meetings with the professors or with student groups, tutoring sessions, after school events, etc., the service requests are more difficult to schedule beforehand.

COLLEGE CLASSES, MAJORS, AND MINORS

Once your Deaf friends are enrolled in college, there are other things to consider. For example, what class do they belong to? Freshman? Junior? Senior? Or what? Learn from MY ASL TUBE:

MY ASL TUBE 4-5: WHAT CLASS ARE YOU?

preparatory student   freshman   sophomore   junior   senior

(Preparatory or "prep" students were a special category of students at Gallaudet who were not considered "real" college students because they lacked crucial skills for success in college. They were required to take remedial courses to repair deficiencies on English, math, science, social studies, and other areas of study. This category has been discontinued, and only older Gallaudet alumni refer to their first class as the prep class.)

graduate student   part-time   full-time

Class levels can be important for Deaf students because many of them are supported financially by Vocational Rehabilitation programs. These programs may try to save money by requiring that Deaf students attend local community colleges for their first two years and then transfer to Gallaudet or NTID or hearing four-year colleges or universities for upper-division courses.

Now, we'll learn all the signs for various majors. We can't list them all because some majors do not have name-signs. As a general rule, the more that Deaf people major in a specific field, the more likely that it will have a name-sign. Everything else is finger-spelled. And be prepared to do a lot of finger-spelling, because Deaf people are majoring in more and more unusual fields. How about paramedic training? Or aviation management? Or viniculture (wine making)? Deaf people have majored in these areas and many more. So, MY ASL TUBE will focus on the most common majors … but be aware that there are many other more exotic majors that Deaf people have pursued.

MY ASL TUBE 4-6: SIGNS FOR COLLEGE MAJORS

Here are all the signs for majors that you learned from MY ASL TUBE:

MAJORS AND MINORS

Major

Minor

undecided

double (major)

MATH AND SCIENCES

math

arithmetic

algebra

geometry

trigonometry

calculus

science

chemistry

biology

physics

earth (science)

engineering

WORLD LANGUAGES

English

French

Spanish

German

Italian

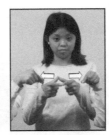

Japanese

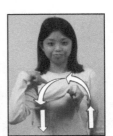

Chinese

VISUAL AND PERFORMING ARTS

art

drawing

painting

sculpture

photography

theater

dance

music

film   video   art history

SOCIAL SCIENCES

psychology   sociology   anthropology   linguistics

SOCIAL STUDIES

American (history)   European (history)   economics   communication

studies

Combine the "studies" sign with various groups:
Deaf Studies
Asian Studies
Black Studies
Hispanic Studies
Latino Studies
LGBT Studies
Women Studies
Etc.

government

various "studies"

BUSINESS AND COMPUTERS

accounting

finance

computer (science/information)

PROFESSIONAL CAREERS

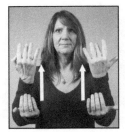
fire (science)

police (science)

cosmetology

dental hygiene

automotive technology

auto body repair

cooking

baking

HUMAN SERVICES

nursing

counseling

education

child development

Let's practice the signs we learned. We'll show a video of a Deaf college student who will tell you about her friends. Watch the video and write down all the information about the friends in the chart.

Friend's Name	Deaf or Hearing?	Class	Major/Minor
1.			
2.			
3.			
4.			
5.			
6.			
7.			
8.			
9.			
10.			
11.			
12.			
13.			
14.			
15.			

MY ASL TUBE 4-7: MY DEAF FRIEND'S CLASSMATES

COLLEGE PEOPLE

You will meet all kinds of people as you make your way through college. You and your Deaf friends can share information about these people, but you need to know the signs for their positions. In the next video, a Deaf person will outline some of the positions at a college or university.

MY ASL TUBE 4-8: PEOPLE AND POSITIONS IN MY COLLEGE OR UNIVERSITY

Here are the signs you learned in the video:

COLLEGE STAFF:

president

professor

teaching assistant

counselor

coach

chairperson
(or coach)

librarian

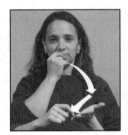
secretary

administrative
assistant

technician

STUDENT OFFICERS (YOU ALREADY KNOW THE SIGN FOR "PRESIDENT" AND "SECRETARY")

vice-president

director

treasurer

parliamentarian

COLLEGE SOCIAL LIFE

There's more to college than classes and majors. For many people, college is the place where they strike out on their own for the first time and it can be an intimidating experience. High school rules are a lot different from college rules. For example, high school students follow a daily schedule while college students have much more flexibility. High school teachers enforce much stricter rules about attendance, homework, etc., while college professors favor more independence for the students. In high school, parents are often heavily involved in their children's education, while in college, parents are not even allowed to find out how their children are doing. It's a whole new ball game and students need to adjust.

They must adjust to a different social life as well. As a college student, they have to navigate their way through a social scene that is filled with a variety of characters. Your Deaf friends also have to navigate but, since they only have limited opportunities to communicate with non-signing hearing students, these Deaf friends will want to gain information from you, a signer, about the hearing college social scene. Likewise, you'll want to learn more about the Deaf college social scene.

One popular topic you'll probably want to share will be about the different kinds of students you and your friends may encounter (or try to avoid). In this case, you need to be able to share your insights about the personal qualities of various people that form the campus scene. Let's learn some new signs that help describe these personal qualities.

You already know some of these qualities because, in Chapter 3, you learned how to explain why you got along or didn't get along with family members. So, to review, let's play a game. On the next page, there are two columns. Column A shows signs for various qualities and column B shows signs for opposite qualities. But the column B qualities are all mixed up, so what you need to do is draw lines from the qualities in A to the opposite qualities in B. Good luck!

MORE PERSONAL QUALITIES

At college, you may encounter people with more diverse qualities than those you find in your extended families. So, let's watch a video and learn signs for additional qualities of people that you might meet on campus. The video will show qualities and their opposites.

MY ASL TUBE 4-9: ADDITIONAL PERSONAL QUALITIES OF COLLEGE STUDENTS

Here are the signs we learned in MY ASL TUBE 4-9:

| calm | anxious/worried | independent | dependent |

lousy ↔ wonderful   clear-headed ↔ confused

serious ↔ mischievous   flexible ↔ strict

open ↔ private/secretive   open-minded ↔ narrow-minded

accommodating ↔ stubborn   awkward ↔ confident

wild/unholy ↔ holy   condescending ↔ admiring

Column A

Column B

Let's put it all together and have a chat with Deaf friends about college staff and student leaders and their personal qualities. In the next video, you'll see these Deaf friends describing campus people and sharing their impressions of them. Watch the video and write down the information you learned in the chart below:

Name	Deaf or Hearing?	Position/relation	Personal Trait
1.			
2.			
3.			
4.			
5.			
6.			
7.			
8.			
9.			
10.			
11.			
12.			
13.			
14.			
15.			

MY ASL TUBE 4-10: COLLEGE AND STUDENT STAFF AND PERSONAL QUALITIES

SIGNS OF THE REAL WORLD

Most ASL students go through culture shock when they try to participate in Deaf world activities. As an ASL student, you may go through a very confusing experience, but you can take heart in knowing that you are not alone—other hearing students go through the same experiences.

Would you be surprised to learn that quite a few Deaf people also go through culture shock when they encounter the Deaf world? One good example is a foreign-born Deaf person who emigrates to the U.S. to pursue a college education. One such Deaf person, Dr. Madan Vasishta, a native of India, shared his "culture shock" experiences in India and the U.S. in an entertaining book, "Deaf in Delhi." Dr. Vasishta became Deaf at the age of eleven and, since there were no schools for Deaf children in his area, he was relegated to the position of cow herder and spent several years tending to his family cattle up in the mountains. It was a lonely experience, which he dealt with by reading westerns.

Fortunately, he discovered a world of Deaf people when he joined a photography club in Delhi. He developed skills in Indian Sign Language and became a leader in the club. Later, some visitors from the United States noted his academic and leadership skills and urged him to apply to Gallaudet University. Miraculously, he gained a scholarship, and in 1967 he boarded a plane for the first time in his life and flew to London, and then to Washington D.C. Let's watch excerpts from his book about what it was like to arrive at Gallaudet as a Deaf country boy from India.

MY ASL TUBE 4-11: EXCERPTS FROM "DEAF IN DELHI"

QUESTIONS:

1. **ARRIVAL AT GALLAUDET:** When Madan arrived in Washington, D.C., what kinds of communication breakdowns did he experience with hearing people and Deaf people? Have you ever had a communication breakdown like this? Please tell us about it.

_____

_____

_____

2. **CLOTHING RULES:** Madan discovered that clothing rules in India were quite different from those in America. Can you describe how American cultural rules concerning clothing caused him a great deal of confusion? Have you ever been confused about clothing rules? How did you deal with the situations?

_____

_____

_____

3. **LOST IN TRANSLATION:** Madan experienced misunderstandings about the meanings of a variety of American words and phrases such as restroom, garage sale, etc. Have you ever had this kind of experience, and, if so, how did you handle the situation?

_____

_____

_____

4. **HUGS AND HANDSHAKES:** What did Madan find confusing about the ways that people greet each other in America? Have you ever had that kind of experience in America or in another country? Tell us about it.

_____

_____

_____

5. **PRIVACY:** Madan had to deal with completely different ideas about privacy between Indian and American culture. How would you describe your own viewpoints about privacy? Are they closer to American or Indian viewpoints? Tell us more.

_____

_____

_____

THE CLASSROOM

SOME DEAF EXPERIENCES IN SCHOOLS, COLLEGES, AND UNIVERSITIES

Now that we know how to chat about all the academic and social aspects of college life, it would be easy to chat with Deaf college or university students about their experiences as they progress toward graduation. Just take classes, move up a grade each year, and graduate. Simple, right? Wrong. College life for many Deaf people is filled with ups and downs and twists and turns. In many cases, Deaf students' family or school experiences may not have prepared them well for college. Their schools may not have provided them with opportunities to develop the knowledge and skills they need to pursue a college education. Or, their families may have overprotected them and, as a result, they may have had few opportunities to make their own decisions. Or, being a Deaf member of a hearing family, none of whom know sign language, may have limited the Deaf college students' awareness of future careers. So they pick a major and career that may not be suited to their temperament and interests. They may go through many changes of academic and career goals until they discover new dreams and ways of thinking that work for them. All in all, Deaf students can go through an anxious, confusing, and sometimes exhilarating time as they pursue a college education and, beyond that, a way of life.

Let's look at the process that several Deaf people went through while pursuing a college education. After you watch each Deaf person's story, write down a summary of the story.

1. _____'s story: _____

_____

_____

_____

2. _____'s story: _____

_____

_____

_____

3. _____'s story: _____

_____

_____

_____

4. _____'s story: _____

_____

_____

_____

5. _____'s Story: _____

_____

_____

_____

MY ASL TUBE 4-12: COLLEGE AND UNIVERSITY TRANSITIONS

Here are some of the signs you learned from MY ASL TUBE

1. _____'s Story:

| doctor | encourage | expensive | course | to pass (course/test) |

Voc. Rehab. all "A's from frosh-senior medical school

(Note: Vocational Rehabilitation (VR) is a program that supports training, education, and careers for disabled people. Many Deaf students receive support from VR for attending college.)

2. _____'s Story:

Decisions Support certificate degree design

3. _____'s Story:

country refused to party to smoke pot

mischief to fail (test/ course) flunked every-thing withdrew

4. _____'s story (finger-spell "birth control" as "B-C" and "sex education" as [S-E-X E-D]):

Hearing ability declined   interactions   strict   private

narrow-minded   accidental pregnancy   go back

5. Billy's story:

oral/oralism   allow   stubborn   expelled   reputation

stuck   can't do anything   envisioned   ironically

Now, let's practice all the things we learned from these five stories narrated by Deaf college students. We'll work in pairs. Partner A will use ASL to tell Partner B a story about his/her high school and college experiences, past, present, and future. Partner B will take notes and then be prepared to retell in ASL the story of Partner A. Then A and B will switch roles with Partner B telling his/her story and Partner A taking notes and then retelling the story. Below is a blank form that Partner A or B can use to take notes.

YOUR STORY: _____

_____

_____

_____

_____

_____

YOUR PARTNER'S STORY: _____

_____

_____

_____

_____

_____

CHOOSING A CAREER

Congratulations! You've navigated the "learning box" and now you're ready for the "work box." Please bear in mind that you will keep on learning things for the rest of your life.

If you're a typical college student, you'll probably go through a stressful period as graduation approaches and you realize you'll be facing the real world in the not-very-distant future. You'll probably be uncertain about what kind of job or career you'll pursue or even if you get a job at all. You've heard horror stories about philosophy majors pumping gas, or chemistry majors serving coffee in cafés because they were not well prepared for a career in their fields.

I guarantee you that your Deaf classmates will be going through even more stressful situations because they must deal with widespread discrimination, both intentional and unintentional. So, to help you and your Deaf friends navigate this difficult and stressful time of life, I'll give you some ASL tools that you can use to support each other through the walking-on-hot-coals-like experience of establishing a career.

There are hundreds of jobs and careers out there, and just winnowing through them all to find the perfect job or career can be an overwhelming experience. To help you explore the job market and narrow down your choices, I'll share with you a way to categorize types of jobs. One way is to divide all the jobs into three general categories: working with 1. People; 2. Things; and 3. Information. This is the traditional approach, but we will need something a lot more precise to determine what kind of career you'll want to pursue. You can organize career categories according to people and environments. There are six categories. Let's watch MY ASL TUBE and learn the categories. As you watch, write down each category and some sample careers.

1. Category: _____. Examples: _____

    _____

    _____

2. Category: _____. Examples: _____

    _____

    _____

3. Category: _____. Examples: _____

    _____

    _____

4. Category: _____. Examples: _____

    _____

    _____

5. Category: _____. Examples: _____

    _____

    _____

6. Category: _____. Examples: _____

    _____

    _____

MY ASL TUBE 4-13: SIX PEOPLE-ENVIRONMENT CATEGORIES WITH EXAMPLES

Here are the signs you learned from MY ASL TUBE:

1. Category . . .; Examples . . .

realistic   carpenter   police officer   fire fighter   mail carrier

2. Category . . .; Examples . . .

investigative   scientist   nurse   doctor   research

3. Category . . .; Examples . . .

artistic   photographer   painter   sculptor   writer

4. Category . . .; Examples . . .

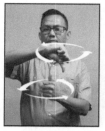
social

teacher

counselor

beautician

social worker

5. Category . . .; Examples . . .

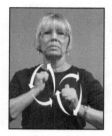
enterprising

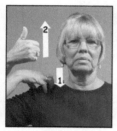
executive/boss

lawyer

director

investor

6. Category . . .; Examples . . .

conventional

secretary

waiter

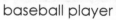
baseball player

Let's practice your newly learned signs. On this page, you'll find a chart with pictures of various careers or professions. In MY ASL TUBE 4-14, you'll meet some Deaf people who will tell you their names and their careers or profession. Write the name of each person in the correct box.

MY ASL TUBE 4-14: DEAF PEOPLE AND THEIR CAREERS AND PROFESSIONS

ASK MISS ASLEY: THE DEAFINITE ANSWER

(Miss ASLey is a Deaf professional etiquettarian. She feels it is her duty to correct uninformed people whenever they make a faux pas about the culture of Deaf people and to show them the proper cultural behavior to exhibit toward the Deaf World. If you want to learn a properly balanced attitude toward Deaf people, Miss ASLey is who you need to consult).

Dear Miss ASLey,

I have been taking ASL for the past two years and I have become friends with other students at my university. I really like one Deaf guy named Joshua who is majoring in biology. I have taken a few classes with him and we have had some great times working on projects together. There is another reason why I take classes with John. I get to watch how John's interpreter translates what the teacher is saying. It really helps my skills.

Joshua has one problem that concerns me—he's too passive. If there is a problem or an argument, I think he gives in too easily. He once shared with me that his family never gave him much support. For example, he didn't get his driver's license until he was 22. Why? His parents thought that Deaf people should not drive. None of his family members could sign, except a few crude or demeaning gestures. One sister tried to communicate with him orally by speaking very slowly and exaggerating her speech sounds. The first time I saw that, I was so embarrassed for Joshua. And I can understand why he can be so passive—he never had any personal power until he left home and came to college.

This semester, Joshua's passivity became a real problem in our English class. The professor for this class, Dr. James Jackson, had a huge attitude problem. On the very first day of class, he spied the sign language interpreter and made a big announcement, for Joshua's benefit, "I am not going to water down this class because we have a Deaf person in it." He was so wrong! Joshua was determined to do the same work as everyone else.

Needless to say, it was a terrible start for the class and people were turned off by the negativity of the hearing professor. Even a few students met Joshua after class and told him what an asshole the professor was. Joshua wanted to switch to another professor but the classes were all full. And Joshua needed the class in order to graduate this semester. So he decided to soldier on.

Since that first class, Professor Jackson made life difficult for Joshua. When Joshua asked the professor to recruit a note-taker, the professor said it was Joshua's responsibility to keep up. Often, the professor handed out reading material and then went right ahead and started talking about the material before Joshua had a chance to at least skim the material. It was impossible for Joshua to read the material and watch the interpreter at the same time. I am sure the professor knew this but he seemed not to care.

To add insult to injury, the professor asked Joshua several times during the semester if he really belonged in the class. Joshua was frustrated but afraid to complain and make the professor angry enough to flunk him. I urged him to go to the disability resources coordinator and ask for help, but he wouldn't go. He was proud that he could succeed in college and told me several times that "Deaf people can do anything that hearing people can do!" He did his best to survive in the class. But the professor's attitude bothered me a lot.

Finally, I decided to do something about this situation. I went to the disability resources coordinator and told her what was happening in the classroom. She was surprised because Joshua never said anything about it. I begged her not to tell him that I had told her about his situation. The coordinator said she would try to find out what was happening with Joshua without getting me involved.

So, a week later, Joshua was moved to a different professor who had had Deaf students before. Jonathan did a lot better, but he found out what I had done and it pissed him off. He said, "I can take care of myself! I'm not a baby!" I told him that maybe I made a mistake not to discuss the issue with him but I was so concerned about the situation that I had to take action. What should I do to restore our friendship?

Anxious Signer

***

Dear Anxious Signer,

By now, you realize that Jonathan is not the passive Deaf person you thought him to be. It is wise to offer help, but wiser not to "take over" the Deaf person's life. I can see that you have a good heart, but you need to let Jonathan experience the consequences of his inaction.

I recommend you apologize to him and promise never to do that again. I make no guarantees that your friendship with Jonathan will be completely restored. Only time will tell. But, at least, he will know that you respect him and, hopefully, he will respect you in turn.

Mannerly,

Miss ASLey

THE ASL CLUB

EXCUSES, EXCUSES, WHO'S GOT EXCUSES

As you travel among the three boxes of life, learning, working, and playing, there are many occasions where Deaf people's plans go SNAFUs (Situation Normal, All Fouled Up). Maybe they were late or missed a class or work assignment or a get-together at the coffee shop. Or maybe they had to leave early or missed a meeting or event.

Deaf people are pretty relaxed about these SNAFUs. In fact, they have invented the expression "DST" which stands for "Deaf Standard Time." Frequently, they will feel a need to explain the situation, since Deaf culture is strongly aligned with sharing information.

Let's learn how to make or understand some common excuses in ASL. You'll find the excuses in the MY ASL TUBE below:

MY ASL TUBE 4-15: COMMON EXCUSES FOR COLLEGE OR UNIVERSITY STUDENTS

Here are some of the excuses you learned in MY ASL TUBE 4-15

SITUATION 1: You were late to school or work.   *POSSIBLE EXCUSES:*

Sorry

I'm

late

car accident

Heavy Traffic

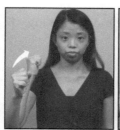

(car) won't start

(car) broke down

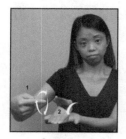
flat tire

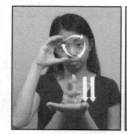
looked for parking...none available

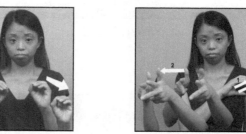
police pulled me over

Lost keys

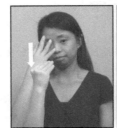

overslept

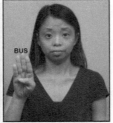

missed bus

dropped kids off at school

SITUATION 2: You missed or will miss a class, work assignment, meeting, etc. (remember to indicate the past or future date first, then the excuse)

I will miss/missed

can't/couldn't come to

POSSIBLE EXCUSES:

class

work

sick

funeral

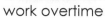

work overtime

vacation

house burned down

flood

alien abduction

SITUATION 3: You must leave early from your class, work, meeting, etc.:

I

must

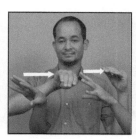

leave

early

POSSIBLE EXCUSES

doctor

lawyer

dentist

appointment

go to   school   to pick up   kid(s)

go to   airport,   pick up   friend

SITUATION 4: You must leave now

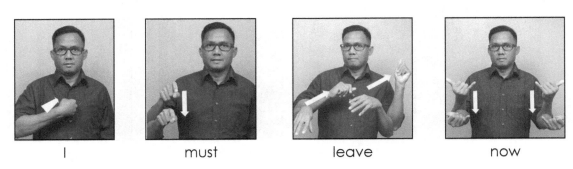

I   must   leave   now

POSSIBLE EXCUSES

I'm sick,   will   throw-up   house   on fire

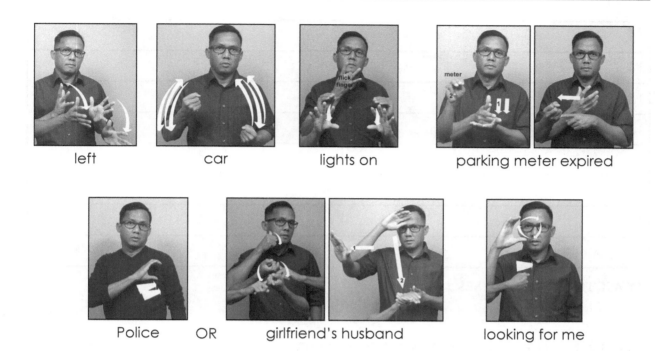

left   car   lights on   parking meter expired

Police   OR   girlfriend's husband   looking for me

Now that we know how to make excuses for different situations, let's watch a MY ASL TUBE video of people making excuses in ASL. Use the information to fill in the following table:

Situation	Excuse
1.	
2.	
3.	
4.	
5.	
6.	
7.	
8.	
9.	
10.	
11.	
12.	

13.	
14.	
15.	
16.	
17.	
18.	
19.	
20.	

MY ASL TUBE 4-16: EXCUSES

DEAF CULTURE CORNER: HEROES AND SHE-ROES

FROM COWHERD TO CHAMPION OF BILINGUAL EDUCATION— THE STORY OF MADAN VASISHTA

Dr. Madan Vasishta was born in 1941 in the tiny village of Gagret located in Himachal Pradesh, a place of natural beauty in the far north of India. At the age of eleven, he became deaf as a result of being afflicted with typhoid and mumps. He also was afflicted with tinnitus, a condition which causes him to hear imaginary loud noises in his heads. Madan found that he was able to manipulate the sounds in his head so that he could "listen" to the music and imaginary sounds brought on by the tinnitis.

Madan's family visited many doctors and he underwent many bizarre treatments to restore his hearing none of which worked. Finally, they gave up and accepted the fact that he would always be deaf. Madan was part of a large extended family and needed a way to communicate with them, since he could not lip-read well. Also, paper and pencil were in short supply in his village so his relatives would "write" what they wanted to tell him in the palm of his hand. It worked to some extent, but it was not always effective.

No schools in his area would accept a deaf student, so Madan studied at home, using the hand-me-down textbooks of his older brother. He taught himself several languages including English, Hindi, and Sanskrit. He also pursued a favorite pastime, reading novels, especially those by authors such as Zane Grey. Amazingly, without any formal schooling after the age of eleven, he was able to pass the Indian national high school examinations at the highest level.

If Madan were hearing, passing the high school examinations would have enabled him to go on to college or to pursue a professional career. But, as a deaf person in a country with virtually no support for deaf people, Madan was unable to find work in a meaningful career. Finally, his father asked him to become a cowherd on the family farm, a demoralizing position for a young man with greater aspirations for his life.

Ten long years passed until, finally, Madan moved to Delhi, where he became a printer's apprentice. Later, he was accepted into a photography school run by the All India Association of the Deaf. It was here that he encountered Deaf people for the first time and learned a new language, Indian Sign Language. This was a life-changing development since he had never met a Deaf person before. Madan learned Indian Sign Language and served as a valuable leader and resource person since he could read, write, and speak English, Hindi, and other languages. He assumed ever more responsible positions within the Deaf community and navigated his way through ever more complex political minefields.

One fortunate day, Madan met a visitor from America, Hester Bennet, who literally changed his life. Hester and Madan had a wonderful visit and, as Hester became more aware of Madan's talents, she asked him if he would consider becoming an undergraduate at Gallaudet College. Madan's initial response was, "What is Gallaudet?" But as he learned more about the World's Only Liberal Arts College (now University) for Deaf people, he became determined to find a way to become part of the Gallaudet community. He faced formidable educational and financial obstacles, but his determination and creative energy led to his acceptance at Gallaudet with a full scholarship.

So, in 1967, a few months after his family had arranged for him to be married to a hearing woman named Nirmala, he left her with his family in India and boarded his first airplane flight ever for London and then Washington, D.C., the locale of Gallaudet College, a place that even a lot of taxi drivers did not know existed. Somehow, he made it to the Gallaudet campus; and there, he realized immediately that he had a lot to learn since he and his classmates could not understand each other. Indian Sign Language and American Sign Language are completely different systems, and even the finger-spelling alphabets are different. Madan also had to navigate considerable cultural differences between American and Indian ways of life. This learning and navigation took up most of his undergraduate years and was the subject of "Deaf in Delhi," a memoir filled with humorous anecdotes about cultural conflicts both in India and in the United States. Some of these anecdotes can be found in Chapter 3 of this book.

Four years later, he graduated with a bachelor's degree in history and psychology. But he had set his sights on something higher. He wanted to become a teacher of the Deaf in India and he realized that he needed a Master's Degree in order to qualify. So, for the next two years, he pursued graduate studies at Gallaudet. In 1973, he became the first Deaf person in Indian history to achieve the prestigious Master of Arts in Teaching Degree from Gallaudet.

With his degree in hand, he had high hopes that he would be able to land a teaching job in India. A few months before graduation, he prepared letters requesting employment at various schools for the Deaf all across India and, with the help of the Indian Embassy in Washington, he mailed the letters to 122 Indian schools for the Deaf. After waiting several months, he received not a single response. It was obvious that none of the schools for the deaf believed in hiring Deaf teachers, even teachers as highly educated and qualified as Madan Vasishta.

Madan had told his many friends that he would soon return to India but, with the rejection of every single application letter, he was forced to follow "Plan B" and apply to schools for the Deaf in the United States. Fortunately, he received a job offer from Kendall Demonstration Elementary School (KDES) on the campus of Gallaudet College. He accepted a position as a social studies teacher in the middle school and thereby began a new chapter in his life.

KDES was supposed to be a model school that other Deaf schools across America could emulate. However, it faced huge problems in educating its Deaf students drawn from the Washington, D.C. area. Most of these students had endured years of neglect as members of poor, hearing families that had few resources for raising deaf children. By the time the children arrived at Kendall at ages six or seven, or even ten years of age, they had few academic skills. Some could not even spell their names. Madan worked with a team of four Deaf and one hearing educator to at least provide their young charges with a decent education. It took all their creativity to break through these years of neglect.

As time passed, with still no job offers from schools for the Deaf in India, Madan continued his work at Kendall School. He also brought his wife, Nirmala, to the U.S. and they started a family.

Despite lack of opportunities in India, he had a dream of making Indian Sign Language a recognized and respected language in India, just like ASL was becoming in America. He solicited the support of Dr. James Woodward and Dr. Kirk Wilson in developing a dictionary of Indian Sign Language. They traveled to India in 1976 where Madan experienced firsthand the discriminatory attitudes against Deaf people. For example, even though Madan was the Principal Investigator of the project, he and his two hearing colleagues were usually introduced as "Dr. Woodward, Dr. Wilson—and the deaf boy from India." On a subsequent project trip, one of the team members challenged Madan, saying, "Why don't you get a PhD? Since there were few Deaf people in the U.S. with doctorates and none in India, Madan resisted the idea initially, but the seed had been planted and gradually took hold.

Madan and his teams had planned four regional dictionaries, and after several years of practical and bureaucratic challenges, the first dictionary of Indian Sign Language in the Delhi region was published in 1980. Three other regional dictionaries were published later by the Gallaudet Research Institute.

The seed that had been planted in the mind of the "deaf boy from India" germinated into a decision to pursue a PhD at Gallaudet University. So, Madan resigned from Kendall School and enrolled once again in the graduate school at Gallaudet. In 1983, he received his PhD in Educational Administration. Confident that his doctorate would open many doors, he sent out letters to all the schools for the Deaf in the U.S. He applied for all sorts of administrative positions: supervising teacher, principal, assistant superintendent, and superintendent. But, as Yogi Berra would say, "It was déjà vu all over again." Just like the situation where he received no response to his application letters to 122 Indian Schools for the Deaf, he received no response to his letters soliciting an administrative position in one of the many schools for the Deaf in the U.S. It was probably for two reasons: (1) In 1983, few schools for Deaf children believed in Deaf people assuming administrative positions, even those with doctorates in educational administration; and (2) Many school administrators were unwilling to hire someone with a strange name and an Indian background even though Dr. Vasishta was now an American citizen.

After recovering from the shock of discovering that the field of Deaf Education was both audist and racist, Madan decided to take on a less exalted administrative position and work his way up the administrative ladder. He got an offer from Victor Galloway, the Deaf superintendent of the Texas School for the Deaf, to become a supervisor of the Middle School program at TSD and after some reluctance, he swallowed his pride and accepted. He had been working as an assistant to the Provost at Gallaudet but once he got out of the "Gallaudet Fish Bowl," he began to advance in his positions and administrative responsibilities. During the five years he was at TSD (1985–90), he advanced to become the Associate Principal. After that period, Dr. Vasishta experienced a rapid rise in his career, and made the moving-van industry richer as he moved from one state to another. In 1990, he became the Assistant Superintendent at the Illinois School for the Deaf and, in 1991, the Superintendent of the East North Carolina School for the Deaf. Because of some serious political problems in North Carolina, Madan left three years later to become superintendent of the New Mexico School for the Deaf where he served for the next six years.

Dr. Vasishta's rapid career advancement was helped by an earth-shaking event that happened in Washington, D.C., in 1988. As you learned in Chapter 1, the Deaf President Now movement at Gallaudet caused both the newly selected hearing President and the hearing Chair of the Board of Trustees to resign to be replaced by the first Deaf president and the first Deaf Chair of the Board in Gallaudet history. The DPN movement was one of the most successful Deaf civil rights campaigns of modern times. It caused many administrators and boards of schools for Deaf children to start recruiting Deaf administrators. After what happened at Gallaudet, who among the Deaf school boards and administrators wanted to be the next site of protests, Madan Vasishta was grateful for the impact of the Deaf President Now movement on his career prospects.

During his years as a teacher and administrator, he became more involved in developing a bilingual education approach as well as a curriculum that helped many Deaf children and youth succeed in school. After six good years as superintendent at NMSD, he retired as superintendent in 1990. Then, it was back to Gallaudet University where, for the next ten years, he used his vast experience to train doctoral students in supervising and administering educational programs. Many of his students advanced to key administrative and executive positions at various schools for the Deaf across the United States.

Madan Vasishta had a full schedule, but this did not stop him from doing some important work in his native country. The Deaf education system in India was chaotic and ineffective. There were no Deaf teachers and most of the hearing teachers were not fluent in Indian Sign Language. To help foster changes in this system, Madan worked with a group of Deaf Indian leaders to establish the Indian Sign Language Research and Training Centre (ISLRT) which opened at the Indira Gandhi National Open University (IGNOU) in 2011. Unfortunately, for the next two years, nothing happened at IGNOU, so the ISLRC was transferred to an agency that was responsible for oral education in India. This was a disaster, since the oral program tried to squeeze ISLRT to death so that oral education could continue unabated.

The Deaf community was up in arms about this terrible turn of events and, with Madan's advice and help, managed a campaign to have ISLRT become an autonomous agency with its own budget and management system. Finally, in 2015, the cabinet of the Prime Minister of India voted to grant this autonomy. ISLRT now hopes to move forward in meeting its dream of improving the lives of Deaf people in India.

Madan has written two memoirs about his experiences, "Deaf in Delhi," and "Deaf in D.C.," which are full of humorous stories and pungent points of view. As we look back on his amazing life, we can see that Deaf people can do anything, even when the odds are heavily stacked against them.

MY ASL TUBE 4-17: THE STORY OF DR. MADAN VASISHTA

HOW DID I DO?

I hope you enjoyed all the things you learned in this chapter. You can use your new skills and knowledge to interact comfortably with Deaf people about their biological and social families. It's a good idea to check your progress. Below are the goals for the chapter along with a continuum from "I did great!" to "I need to work on this more." Write an "x" in the place that you feel reflects your progress in this chapter.

Now that you have finished Chapter 4, you, the student, can use ASL to:

1. Describe the process involved in applying to and enrolling in a college or university.

⟵——————————————————————————————⟶

I need to work on this more   I did great!

2. Demonstrate correct usage of auxiliary verbs in ASL.

⟵——————————————————————————————⟶

I need to work on this more   I did great!

3. Outline some of the support services offered to Deaf and hard of hearing students.

⟵——————————————————————————————⟶

4. Identify some majors and minors, as well as courses and classes, and the process by which students complete their education.

⟵——————————————————————————————⟶

I need to work on this more   I did great!

5. Outline some of the staff and student positions at a college or university.

⟵——————————————————————————————⟶

I need to work on this more   I did great!

6. Describe some personal qualities that you find among members of the campus community.

⟵——————————————————————————————⟶

I need to work on this more   I did great!

7. Analyze some of the Culture Shock issues raised by the experiences of Dr. Madan Vasishta when he first became a student at Gallaudet University.

⟵——————————————————————————————⟶

I need to work on this more   I did great!

8. Summarize some typical mini-biographies of Deaf college or university students and compare them to their own autobiographies.

I need to work on this more   I did great!

9. Discuss what it means to be a hearing or Deaf ally of Deaf college students.

I need to work on this more   I did great!

10. Outline and give examples of some of the major categories of careers.

I need to work on this more   I did great!

11 Make excuses or give reasons for not meeting your school or work obligations.

I need to work on this more   I did great!

12. Outline the Life Story of Dr. Madan Vasishta, Deaf Indian Education Pioneer.

I need to work on this more   I did great!

CHAPTER 5

Living in the "Working and Playing Boxes" of the Deaf World

INTRODUCTION TO THE CHAPTER

In the previous chapter, we explored the life process of learning, particularly the process of getting a college education. With this new information and these new skills, you'll be able to chat comfortably with your Deaf classmates about all aspects of school, college, or university life.

After you complete your college education, you move into the next "box" of life: working. Once you've gained skills in communicating about pursuing a career, you'll be able to chat comfortably with any Deaf person, be it classmate, coworker, or any other co-person.

Finally, you can anticipate retiring from your career and entering the third "box of life": playing or leisure time activities. You'll need skills in communicating in ASL about the many "playing" activities in this box of life.

So, this chapter will provide you with the tools for communicating about your working and playing activities. After you complete Chapter 5, you'll be able to use ASL to:

1. **Describe the process involved in choosing a career and applying for and starting a new job.**

2. **Modify signs to indicate daily, weekly, monthly, and annual routines as well as routines with more general time lines.**

3. **Discuss personal qualities that you find among people at work.**

4. **Describe some of the employment positions that Deaf people encounter in the world of work.**

5. **Use some common finger-spelled abbreviations in the working world to communicate with Deaf employees.**

6. **Summarize some typical mini-biographies of Deaf people in the world of work and compare them to their own autobiographies.**

7. **Use non-manual markers (NMMs) to create conditional sentences that are used in the world of work or in other situations.**

8. **Demonstrate how to ask for help or favors using intimate/casual, formal, and pleading approaches.**

9. **Describe some categories of activities that Deaf people are prone to engage in during retirement.**

10. **Outline some of the ways that Deaf people deal with dying or death as part of life in the Deaf world.**

11. **Describe how Deaf people can create ASL literature and folklore as exemplified by ABC and number stories.**

12. **Describe the life and achievements of a Deaf Actress and ASL poetess, Dorothy Squire Miles.**

THE CLASSROOM

GETTING A JOB AND STARTING A CAREER

Once you've figured out what kind of job or career you want, and once you've completed the necessary academic qualifications, the next step is actually securing a job. It may not be the job or career you were hoping for, but perhaps you'll leapfrog from job to job until you find your longed-for career.

With Deaf people, the process can sometimes be more chaotic. For example, when I went to Gallaudet College in the 1960s, the most common career choice for Deaf graduates was to become a teacher at a school for the Deaf. Often Gallaudet graduates had to teach in fields that were completely different from the field they had majored in. I was not sure about my major, and there was no career counseling in those days, so my classmates tried to give me the best career advice they could. I had very good English, so my friends suggested that I major in math.

"Why?" I asked.

"Well," they said, "Most Deaf schools will asked you to teach a subject that you didn't major in. So, why not major in math? Then, it'll be easier to get a job because you can teach either English or Math.

So, I majored in math and, soon after graduation, I was hired by a school for the Deaf … to teach social studies!

Your Deaf friends can expect a lot of surprises as they look for their first job after graduating from college. Deaf people face real challenges: Access to information about available jobs can be difficult to find; Interviews can be a hassle because the employer may not understand the Deaf candidate; human resource directors may not see the value of an interpreter and many other roadblocks. Even when an interview is secured, the hiring people may fall back on certain ways to block Deaf employees, such as "The job requires use of a telephone." This excuse is becoming more and more irrelevant since more and more communications are conducted by e-mail and since sign-to-voice relay services are readily available.

Your Deaf friends will be happy to share the triumphs and tribulations of the working world with you. Let's watch some stories about Deaf people and the different situations they faced as they pursued their careers. After you finish watching each story, write down the name of the story-teller and the details of his or her career.

MY ASL TUBE 5-1: STORIES ABOUT APPLYING FOR WORK

1. _____'s story: _____

   _____

   _____

   _____

2. _____'s story: _____

_____

_____

_____

3. _____'s story: _____

_____

_____

_____

4. _____'s story: _____

_____

_____

_____

5. _____'s story: _____

_____

_____

_____

Here are some of the signs you learned from MY ASL TUBE.

1. _____'s Story:

new place

west

develop

resume

volunteer

experience

to inform me

qualified

to hire

2. _____'s Story: ("company" is abbreviated "C-O"):

intern

company

create/invent

planned

worried

access

e-mail

VRS

variety

3. _____'s Story:

read a lot

analytic skills

dramas

law (school)

searched a lot

referred

make a face

doubtful

discrimination

(job) restructuring

4. _____'s Story:

only one

involved

my own

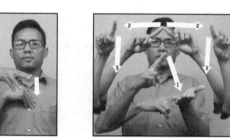
contract

challenge

communication
breakdown

better and
better

production assistant

5. _____'s Story:

community college

TV advertisement

peace

sent

to pick me

Now, let's practice all the things we learned from these five stories. We'll work in pairs. Partner A will use ASL to tell Partner B a story about his/her experience in preparing for and securing a job or pursuing a career. Partner B will take notes and be prepared to tell the story of Partner A to the class. Then A and B will switch roles. If either partner does not have a job or a career yet, he/she should make one up. Below is a blank form that Partner A or B can use to take notes.

YOUR STORY: _____

_____

_____

_____

_____

_____

YOUR PARTNER'S STORY: _____

_____

_____

_____

_____

_____

LINGUISTIC ILLUMINATIONS

MODIFYING SIGNS TO INDICATE DAILY, WEEKLY, MONTHLY, AND ANNUAL ROUTINES

Whether you work full-time or part-time, your job will require you to follow schedules and routines. You already know how to communicate about past, present, and futures, dates and times. Now we need to learn how to communicate the details of routines.

ASL has wonderful linguistic features that enable you to modify signs to show daily, weekly, monthly and annual routines. These features follow the logical extension of various calendars in a way that makes sense. Watch MY ASL TUBE and you'll see what I mean.

MY ASL TUBE 5-2: LEARNING DAILY, WEEKLY, MONTHLY, AND ANNUAL ROUTINES

Here are the signs we learned:

DAILY ROUTINES:

every day   every morning   every noon   every afternoon   every evening

WEEKLY ROUTINES:

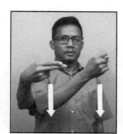
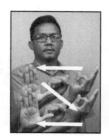

Every Mon, Wed, & Fri.   Every Tues. & Thurs.   every weekend   once a week

twice a week   every week   every two weeks   every six weeks

MONTHLY ROUTINES

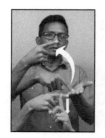

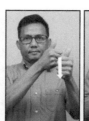
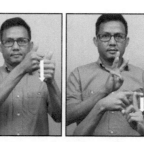

once a month   twice a month   every month   (every) six months

ANNUAL ROUTINES

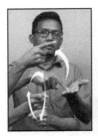     

| once a year | twice a year | every year | every two years | every ten years |

Let's practice what we learned. On the next page, you'll find a one-year calendar. In MY ASL TUBE, you'll see various people describing in ASL the routines that they follow. Write in the routines on the calendar. For example, the person in the video might say, "In January, every Monday and Thursday, we throw out the trash." You can write in the routines on the January calendar. This exercise is challenging but fun.

This Year

JANUARY

Sun	Mon	Tue	Wed	Thu	Fri	Sat
					1	2
3	4	5	6	7	8	9
10	11	12	13	14	15	16
17	18	19	20	21	22	23
24	25	26	27	28	29	30
31						

FEBRUARY

Sun	Mon	Tue	Wed	Thu	Fri	Sat
	1	2	3	4	5	6
7	8	9	10	11	12	13
14	15	16	17	18	19	20
21	22	23	24	25	26	27
28	29					

MARCH

Sun	Mon	Tue	Wed	Thu	Fri	Sat
		1	2	3	4	5
6	7	8	9	10	11	12
13	14	15	16	17	18	19
20	21	22	23	24	25	26
27	28	29	30	31		

APRIL

Sun	Mon	Tue	Wed	Thu	Fri	Sat
					1	2
3	4	5	6	7	8	9
10	11	12	13	14	15	16
17	18	19	20	21	22	23
24	25	26	27	28	29	30

MAY

Sun	Mon	Tue	Wed	Thu	Fri	Sat
1	2	3	4	5	6	7
8	9	10	11	12	13	14
15	16	17	18	19	20	21
22	23	24	25	26	27	28
29	30	31				

JUNE

Sun	Mon	Tue	Wed	Thu	Fri	Sat
			1	2	3	4
5	6	7	8	9	10	11
12	13	14	15	16	17	18
19	20	21	22	23	24	25
26	27	28	29	30		

JULY

Sun	Mon	Tue	Wed	Thu	Fri	Sat
					1	2
3	4	5	6	7	8	9
10	11	12	13	14	15	16
17	18	19	20	21	22	23
24	25	26	27	28	29	30
31						

AUGUST

Sun	Mon	Tue	Wed	Thu	Fri	Sat
	1	2	3	4	5	6
7	8	9	10	11	12	13
14	15	16	17	18	19	20
21	22	23	24	25	26	27
28	29	30	31			

SEPTEMBER

Sun	Mon	Tue	Wed	Thu	Fri	Sat
				1	2	3
4	5	6	7	8	9	10
11	12	13	14	15	16	17
18	19	20	21	22	23	24
25	26	27	28	29	30	

OCTOBER

Sun	Mon	Tue	Wed	Thu	Fri	Sat
						1
2	3	4	5	6	7	8
9	10	11	12	13	14	15
16	17	18	19	20	21	22
23	24	25	26	27	28	29
30	31					

NOVEMBER

Sun	Mon	Tue	Wed	Thu	Fri	Sat
		1	2	3	4	5
6	7	8	9	10	11	12
13	14	15	16	17	18	19
20	21	22	23	24	25	26
27	28	29	30			

DECEMBER

Sun	Mon	Tue	Wed	Thu	Fri	Sat
				1	2	3
4	5	6	7	8	9	10
11	12	13	14	15	16	17
18	19	20	21	22	23	24
25	26	27	28	29	30	31

MY ASL TUBE 5-3: WRITING ROUTINES INTO A CALENDAR

NON-SPECIFIC TIME LINES

Your work routines may not always be as specific as you would like. There are many non-specific signs that are used to describe how often people perform various activities. Watch MY ASL TUBE and learn more about these signs:

MY ASL TUBE 5-4: DESCRIBING NON-SPECIFIC ROUTINES/PATTERNS OF ACTIVITIES

Below is a continuum line that shows the signs for various non-specific characteristic adverbs from "always" to "never."

    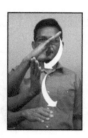

(≈100% of the time) (≈80–99% of the time) (≈15–79% of the time) (≈5–14% of the time) (0% of the time)

Practice these new signs until they become second nature.

DEAF COFFEE NIGHT

GETTING ALONG WITH PEOPLE AT WORK

As a new employee in your place of work, you'll come in contact with a wide variety of people. Naturally, some of these people will be a pleasure to spend time with; others may be persons to avoid. Your Deaf colleagues may have good information about the people at your workplace. They'll want to help you succeed by telling you privately about personal characteristics and work habits of the workers they know. You already learned some personal qualities of family members in Chapter 3. Let's review the qualities and their opposites:

rich ↔ poor	young ↔ old	strong ↔ weak	humble ↔ famous/arrogant
polite ↔ rude	sweet ↔ grouchy	friendly ↔ snobbish	appropriate ↔ weird/strange
	ugly ↔ pretty/beautiful/handsome/cute		

We also learned some personal qualities of people we might come in contact with at our school, college, or university. Let's review these qualities:

anxious/worried ↔ calm   dependent ↔ independent   wonderful ↔ lousy

confused ↔ clear-headed   mischievous ↔ serious   strict ↔ flexible

private/secretive ↔ open   narrow-minded ↔ open-minded   stubborn ↔ accommodating

confident ↔ awkward   holy ↔ wild/unholy   superior ↔ admiring

Now, we'll learn some personal qualities that you might find among your co-workers.

MY ASL TUBE 5-5: PERSONAL AND WORK QUALITIES OF PEOPLE AT WORK

Here are the signs we learned in MY ASL TUBE 5-5:

PERSONAL QUALITIES:

good   bad   outgoing   shy

kind   mean/cruel   wise   ignorant/stupid

smart   pea-size brain   dumb   idiot

WORK HABITS:

| hard-working | ↔ | lazy | alert | ↔ | sleepy |

| fast | ↔ | slow | on-time | ↔ | late |

| careful | ↔ | careless | responsible | ↔ | irresponsible |

POSITIONS IN A COMPANY OR ORGANIZATION

Just as you discovered the signs for various positions of faculty, staff, and students in a college or university, you'll find there are also signs for positions in a company, organization or agency. Let's watch MY ASL TUBE and discover some of these positions.

MY ASL TUBE 5-6: POSITIONS YOU MAY FIND IN A COMPANY OR ORGANIZATION

Here are the positions you saw in MY ASL TUBE:

Finger-spelled positions: Chief Executive Officer = CEO; Chief Financial Officer = CFO; Chief Operations Officer = COO.

Director/Manager   Boss   Supervisor   Coordinator

Coworker   Admin. Assistant   Board   Member

Let's play a game. Imagine you are on the hiring committee for a big company. You must fill eight positions out of fifteen people who have applied. You need to base your decision on the personal qualities or work traits that you discover during the interview. Based on each applicant's, decide whether or not to hire the applicant. Good luck!

Name	Position	Personal/Work Trait	Hire or Not?
1.			
2.			
3.			
4.			
5.			
6.			
7.			
8.			
9.			
10.			
11.			

12.			
13.			
14.			
15.			

MY ASL TUBE 5-7: JOB INTERVIEWS AND HIRING DECISIONS

FINGER-SPELLING FINESSE

FINGER-SPELLED ABBREVIATIONS

When you finally get hired and start working for your new company or organization or agency or school, you may find opportunities to interact with Deaf people at your workplace. You'll often find that their conversations are dotted with abbreviations.

To help you carry out some great conversations with your Deaf coworkers, we will show you some of the common abbreviations they use. There are many abbreviations and we can't show you them all, but we can show you the most common ones. Also, we'll put the abbreviations in categories instead of listing them all alphabetically. Why? Because if you and your Deaf coworker are talking about some issue or topic, you'll be able to use context to identify the finger-spelled word. Here's the list:

Addresses: AVE=avenue, BLVD=boulevard, RD=road, ST=street

Money: CASH, CENTS, CHECK, OT = overtime, RENT, SALE

Time: HRS=hours, MIN=minute(s), SEC=second(s)

Weight and Dimensions: MG=milligrams, OZ=ounce(s), LBS=pounds; MM=millimeter(s), CM=centimeter(s), KM=kilometer(s), INCH(ES), FEET, YARD(S) , MILE(S), PT = pint(s), QT = quart(s), GAL = gallon(s),

Media: I-PAD, MAC, PC, HD = hard drive, FB = Facebook, EMAIL

Office equipment: AC = air conditioning, JUNK, USED

Office Divisions: CO = company, DEPT = department, FIX, TAX, ID= identification

Transportation: BUS, CAR, CAB, TAXI, GAS, OIL

Qualities: EASY, EARLY, LATE, LUCKY, NG = no good, STYLE, FRESH, SAFE, SEXY, TB = too bad, UPSET, FAV = favorite, HC = handicapped, SLOW

Places: BANK, PARK, BEACH, BBQ = barbecue

Now, let's practice using these finger-spelled words and abbreviations in conversations in the workplace. In "MY ASL TUBE," different people will tell you different things or ask you different questions. Each of their statements or questions will contain a finger-spelled word or abbreviation. In the chart below, write down what the person in your workplace signed and the word or words that he/she finger-spelled. Remember to use the context to help you understand the finger-spelling.

What did the person at work say or ask?	Finger-Spelled Word(s)
1.	
2.	
3.	
4.	
5.	
6.	
7.	
8.	
9.	
10.	
11.	
12.	
13.	
14.	
15.	

MY ASL TUBE 5-8: SOME FINGER-SPELLED WORDS IN A WORK ENVIRONMENT

THE ASL CLUB

SOME WORK-LIFE STORIES

So far, we've learned signs that will help us communicate with Deaf people about choosing a career, applying for a job, communicating in the workplace, etc. Now, we will learn about what happens over the working life of Deaf people from the time they are hired to the time they retire. We'll see stories about the work life and experiences of three Deaf people. Watch their stories and use the information to write a short biography of each.

1. _____'s story: _____

_____

_____

_____

_____

2. _____'s story: _____

_____

_____

_____

_____

3. _____'s story: _____

_____

_____

_____

_____

MY ASL TUBE 5-9: THREE DEAF WORKERS' STORIES

Here are some of the signs you learned by watching these Deaf work-life stories:

1. _____'s Story:

superintendent

to be patient

fed up

to quit

to transfer

sponsor

to be promoted

principal

to retire

to look back on

2. _____'s Story:

barely

money management

transportation

part-time

bagger

to survive

drunk

to be jailed

tough

responsibility

3. _____'s Story:

gestures

to stay hidden

immigrant

attitude

to look down on me

to put together

to be laid off

to pay me

to suspend

insurance

ASL IN YOUR FACE

USING NMMS TO CREATE CONDITIONAL SENTENCES RELATED TO WORK

When you work with Deaf co-workers or administrators, you and your Deaf colleagues will often need to communicate specific details of the job to each other. Perhaps you will need to share some rules or make a prediction about situations and their consequences or even make an ironic comment about the culture of your workplace.

One of the most common sentence forms that you may use for these purposes is a conditional sentence. For example:

Factual detail: *If the temperature goes below 32 degrees, water will freeze.*
Prediction: *If it rains tomorrow, the picnic will be cancelled.*
Ironic: *If I could win the lottery, I would quit this job.*

ASL conditional sentences are similar to their English counterparts, with one exception. In English sentences, the conditional clause can happen either before or after the main clause. For example, you can either say:

1. *"If it rains, the picnic will be cancelled."*

OR

2. *"The picnic will be cancelled if it rains."*

Most ASL sentences are based on real-time events, so sentence 1 will work just fine in ASL since first, it may rain and, if that happens, then, second, the picnic will be cancelled. But sentence 2, which reverses the conditional and main clauses, will violate ASL's real-time sequence since it doesn't make sense that, first, the picnic will be cancelled and then, second, it will rain. So, in ASL, always put the conditional clause first and the main clause second.

In English, you usually start a conditional clause with the word "If," in ASL, you can express "If" in three different ways. Let's watch MY ASL TUBE and learn how to produce these three conditional clauses. We'll show three versions of "If it rains, the picnic will be cancelled."

MY ASL TUBE 5-10: THREE WAYS TO CREATE CONDITIONAL CLAUSES

Here are the three ways that ASL is used to form conditional clauses:

1. NMM only

2. NMM + "suppose"

3. NMM + "If"

Now, let's practice conditional sentences which you might see a Deaf person make. Watch MY ASL TUBE and use the information to write the Conditional Clause and the Consequent or Main Clause for each sentence:

Conditional Clause	Consequence or Main Clause
1.	
2.	
3.	
4.	
5.	
6.	
7.	
8.	
9.	

10.	
11.	
12.	
13.	
14.	
15.	

MY ASL TUBE 5-11: EXAMPLES OF CONDITIONAL SENTENCES IN WORK PLACES

THE ASL CLUB

ASKING FOR HELP OR FAVORS

In a variety of situations at college, in the work place, or at a social club, you will find that Deaf people can be very helpful. It is easy to ask them for their assistance. However, you need to know that there are different levels of communication such as casual, formal, and pleading, and you need to know which level to use when asking for help or favors. Watch MY ASL TUBE to see how this works.

MY ASL TUBE 5-12: HOW TO ASK FOR HELP OR FAVORS

Here are the signs you learned that you can use to ask for help or favors. Suppose you asked someone to wash the dishes. Here are the levels you would use:

Casual/Intimate: Used with a spouse, close friend or family member. This request is normally granted.

 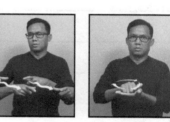

(get attention) ...   dishes   wash.

Formal A: Used with someone with equal or higher status who may or may not accept the request.

Please...   dishes   wash

Formal B: Same as Formal A but "for me" is added.
English: "Please wash the dishes for me"
ASL "Please, for me, dishes wash."

Please   for me....   dishes   wash

Pleading: Used with someone much higher in status who might be reluctant to help.
English: "Do you mind washing the dishes?"

Do you mind...   dishes   wash?

What are some favors or help that we might ask of a person? You can find a lot of them in Chapter 2 under chores and routines.

Let's practice asking for help or favors of a person. Watch MY ASL TUBE and use the information to complete the table below. You need to write the level of formality and the favor requested. You have a choice of Casual, Formal A ("please"), Formal B ("please, for me"), and Pleading:

Level of Formality	Favor/Help Being Requested
1.	
2.	
3.	
4.	
5.	
6.	
7.	
8.	
9.	
10.	

11.	
12.	
13.	
14.	
15.	
16.	

MY ASL TUBE 5-13: EXAMPLES OF ASKING FOR HELP OR FAVORS

ASKING FOR ADVICE ON WHAT TO WEAR

In the Deaf World, you may not be sure about the "dress code" for various events. Deaf people may be more casual in their attire, or just as formal as hearing people. So, we'll play a game of "*OH DEAR! WHAT SHALL I WEAR???*" Work with a partner and ask him/her what to wear at any of the following situations. Your partner should describe an outfit that is appropriate for the situation. Here are possible situations:

OH DEAR! WHAT SHALL I WEAR?..

1. **TO THE PROM**

2. **ON THE FARM**

3. **AT THE BEACH**

4. **AT THE SKI RESORT**

5. **ON AN OCEAN CRUISE**

6. **AT A WEDDING**

7. **AT A SLUMBER PARTY**

8. **AT THE COUNTY FAIR**

9. **AT A FUNERAL**

10. **AT A CHRISTMAS/HANNUKAH PARTY**

11. **ON NEW YEAR'S EVE**

12. **AT A HALLOWEEN PARTY**

THE DEAF CLUB

LEISURE TIME ACTIVITIES

As Richard Bolles pointed out, we need to extricate ourselves from three rigid boxes of life: The box of learning from 0–20ish; the box of working from 20ish to 65ish; and the box of playing from 65ish to death. Instead, we need to participate in all three types of activities throughout our lives.

Let's learn how to communicate about playing or leisure-time activities. It's vital that we be aware that these activities are not limited to the elder years. However, when people reach retirement age, they may have a lot more time for these activities. Some people never actually retire because they are having so much fun in new projects or activities. Others may have a difficult time making the transition from a world where work is a primary focus to a world where there is no work to deal with.

It probably would not be necessary to have a section on leisure-time activities because, in Chapter 1, we learned of the numerous ways that Deaf people celebrate being Deaf. There is a lot of "play" activities going on in clubs, sports teams, alumni associations, churches, and wherever else Deaf people get together for learning, playing, and working.

However, there are some activities that seem to predominate in the time frame of retirement. That is because retired people's time lines are not as structured as they were during their youthful years when teachers and parents dictated how time would be spent, or during their working years when they had to put in their "40 hours" a week.

For some Deaf people, retirement may be like paradise at first, since almost no one can tell you what to do and when to do it. But some people need more structure in their lives. They need to feel they are making progress toward some goals, rather than just sitting around watching "Jeopardy" and "Wheel of Fortune." For other Deaf people, retirement may seem an even busier life than when they were working. Their activities are extensive and varied.

If you'd want to organize all these myriad retirement activities, I recommend a system I've developed called S-C-H-I-E-F-S. This acronym stands for: Spiritual, Creative, Healthy, Intellectual, Errands, Financial, and Social Activities. Watch MY ASL TUBE and learn about these categories and their activities.

MY ASL TUBE 5-14: SOME CATEGORIES OF ACTIVITIES DURING RETIREMENT

Here are the categories and activities that you learned about in MY ASL TUBE 5-14:

SPIRITUAL

Note: In Chapter 1, you already learned the signs for Church, Temple, Mosque, Religion, Catholic, Baptist, Methodist, Lutheran, Mormon, Buddhist, Jewish, and Muslim.

Some other concepts are finger-spelled: Yoga, Koran, and Imam.

General Concepts

God

spiritual

meditation

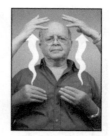
enlightenment

Religious Leaders

priest

nun

preacher

rabbi

Judeo-Christian Tools and Concepts

bible

old testament

new testament

Heaven

Hell

CREATIVE AND CULTURAL:

You have already learned about hobbies and other creative activities in Chapter 1. One creative activity that we haven't focused on yet is travel. Here's what you learned in MY ASL TUBE:

| travel (version 1) | travel (version 2) | group tour | cruise |

HEALTHY LIVING:

You have already learned about sports and recreation in Chapter 1 and about personal hygiene in Chapter 2. Here are a few more terms related to healthy living from MY ASL TUBE:

| physical training | independent living | assisted living | nursing home |

INTELLECTUAL:

You have already learned about educational programs in Chapter 4. Here are a few more signs that can expand your awareness of possibilities for intellectual growth.

| retreat | study group | to think/ponder | to analyze |

ERRANDS OR DAY-TO-DAY ACTIVITIES

You have already learned most of the signs for errands and day-to-day activities in Chapter 2. Here are a few more that often are a part of the retired person's daily life.

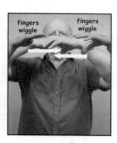

| organizing | renovating | downsizing | simple | complex |

FINANCIAL:

You have already learned some financial status signs such as "rich" and "poor." Also, things like Social Security (S-S), "stocks" and "bonds" are finger-spelled. Here are more signs:

| average | comfortable | pension | investing | finance |

SOCIAL

Here are some specific signs that you can use when chatting about social activities:

| socializing | sharing | supporting | volunteering | taking care of |

SOME STORIES ABOUT DEAF RETIREE'S EXPERIENCES

Let's learn about four Deaf individuals and what their lives were like after they retired. We'll learn that each person's experiences are different, but also similar because they maintained their connections within the Deaf community. Watch their stories and use the information to write a short biography.

1. _____'s story: _____

_____

_____

_____

2. _____'s story: _____

_____

_____

_____

3. _____'s story: _____

_____

_____

_____

4. _____'s story: _____

_____

_____

_____

MY ASL TUBE 5-15: FOUR DEAF RETIREES' STORIES

THE DEAF WAY OF LIFE AND DEATH

We are all aware of (or try to ignore) the fact that every person's life eventually comes to an end. Since members and friends of the Deaf community value each other, the community will come together to grieve and say farewell when a community member dies. If you, the ASL student, have developed a great relationship with the Deaf community, you'll be asked to join the grieving for that person's death and the celebration of that person's life. These are good opportunities to mix with Deaf people and cement your positive relationship with them as an ally. Naturally, you'll need to know some signs related to death and dying as well as grieving and the celebration of a life. Watch the next MY ASL TUBE for these signs:

MY ASL TUBE 5-16: SOME SIGNS RELATED TO LIFE AND DEATH

Here are the signs you learned in this video:

DEATH AND DYING:

Some words are finger-spelled such as "cancer," "dying," and "hospice."

Alzheimer's

health deteriorating

bedridden

vigil

to die, died

passed away

dead/gone

donated

POST-MORTEM RITUALS

funeral

memorial
(service)

celebration
(of life)

bury, burial

cremated/ion

COMMON CONDOLENCES AND CLICHÉS

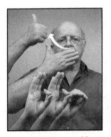

better off

(in a) **better place**

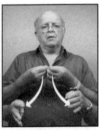

(I am sorry for your) **loss**

(I will) **miss** (him/her)

During the memorial service or celebration of life, various speakers will talk about the qualities of the person who died. A lot of emotions will arise, both from the people at the service and also in reference to the person they are celebrating. It's a good idea to review all the emotions and qualities that you learned in this chapter.

Here are some qualities of friends and family (Chapter 3):

rich ↔ poor	young ↔ old	strong ↔ weak	humble ↔ famous/arrogant
polite ↔ rude	sweet ↔ grouchy	friendly↔ snobbish	appropriate ↔ weird/strange
	ugly ↔ pretty/beautiful/handsome/cute		

Here are the qualities of people at your school, college, or university (Chapter 4):

anxious/worried ↔ calm	dependent ↔ independent	wonderful ↔ lousy
confused ↔ clear-headed	mischievous ↔ serious	strict ↔ flexible
private/secretive ↔ open	narrow-minded ↔ open-minded	stubborn ↔ accommodating
confident ↔ awkward	holy ↔ wild/unholy	superior ↔ admiring

Here are the qualities you found in the working world (Chapter 5):

good ↔ bad	outgoing ↔ shy	kind ↔ mean/cruel	wise ↔ ignorant/stupid
fast ↔ slow	on-time ↔ late	careful ↔ careless	responsible ↔ irresponsible
smart ↔ pea-size brain/dumb/idiot/stupid		Hard-working ↔ lazy	alert ↔ sleepy

To round out your repertoire of qualities, here are some examples of qualities that might be used in a eulogy or a memorial:

MY ASL TUBE 5-17: SOME ADDITIONAL SIGNS FOR VARIOUS EMOTIONS AND QUALITIES

Here are the signs you learned in MY ASL TUBE:

PERSONAL QUALITIES

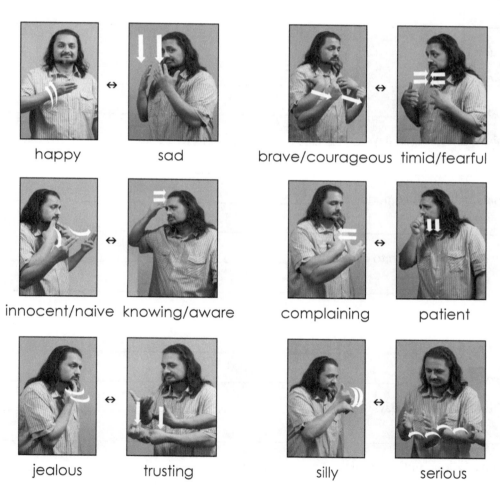

happy	sad	brave/courageous	timid/fearful
innocent/naive	knowing/aware	complaining	patient
jealous	trusting	silly	serious

Now, let's imagine that three beloved members of the Deaf community have passed away. You will be attending a funeral, a memorial service, and a celebration of life for each of these people. A Deaf leader will give a eulogy at each ceremony. Watch MY ASL TUBE and use the information from the video to respond to questions about the deceased person's life.

Here are the questions:

1. Maurice:

    Type of ceremony: _____

    Cause of death: _____

    How he spent his final days: _____

    _____

    Personal qualities and emotions: _____

    _____

    Eulogy speaker's relation to deceased: _____

    _____

2. Caroline:

    Type of ceremony: _____

    Cause of death: _____

    How she spent her final days: _____

    _____

    Personal qualities and emotions: _____

    _____

    Eulogy speaker's relation to deceased: _____

    _____

3. Roger:

    Type of ceremony: _____

    Cause of death: _____

    How he spent his final days: _____

    _____

    Personal qualities and emotions: _____

    _____

    Eulogy speaker's relation to deceased: _____

    _____

MY ASL TUBE 5-18: THREE EULOGIES

SIGNS OF THE REAL WORLD

Deaf Literature is a rich and diverse collection of ways that Deaf people can explore their own culture as well as create artistic expression using ASL. However, the field of Deaf literature has been muddied by the participation of hearing writers who create their own interpretation of the Deaf experience. Often the interpretations do not match the reality of the Deaf experience. For this reason, I will put these works in a special category: hearing interpretations of Deaf or hearing literature. Works in this category include "The Heart is a Lonely Hunter" (novel and film); virtually all songs interpreted into sign language; and other stories and shows created by hearing writers and performing artists.

Deaf literature is a distinct category with several genres

1. Poetry, novels, biographies and other forms of literature about Deaf people written in English. Examples: "They Say I am Deaf," poem by Saul N. Kessler; "You Have to be Deaf to Understand," poem by Willard J. Madsen; numerous biographies and autobiographies by various Deaf authors.

2. Theater works developed by Deaf playwrights and performed in sign language. Examples, "A Play of Our Own" by Dorothy Miles, "Sign Me Alice" by Gilbert C Eastman; "The Hearing Test" by Willy Conley. "A Deaf Family Diary" by Don Bangs, Sequels to "A Play of Our Own" by Steven Baldwin, and other playwrights.

3. Poems designed to be performed in ASL. Examples, "Seasons" by Dot Miles; "Dandelions" by Clayton Valli; "The Treasure" by Ella Mae Lentz, and others.

4. Deaf Jokes which you can find in the "My ASL Book" series.

5. A-B-C alphabet and 1-2-3 numbers stories, a unique form of literature which tells a story using the letters of the alphabet or numbers. This form of literature is so unique that we need to show you examples in My ASL Tube.

MY ASL TUBE 5-19: AN ALPHABET STORY AND A NUMBERS STORY

Did you enjoy the stories? Here is a challenge for you: write down the elements of each story represented by the letters of the alphabet from A – Z and the numbers from 1 to 10.

A_____; B_____; C_____; D_____; E_____

F_____; G_____; H_____; I_____; J_____

K_____; L_____; M_____; N_____; O_____

P_____; Q_____; R_____; S_____; T_____

U_____; V_____; W_____; X_____; Y_____

Z_____

Now try the numbers story:

1_____; 2_____; 3_____; 4_____; 5_____

6_____; 7_____; 8_____; 9_____; 10_____

Perhaps you can work with a Deaf friend and create your own stories. Or Google "ABC Stories in ASL." You will be amazed at all the creativity of the sign artists.

DEAF HEROES AND SHE-ROES

DOROTHY SQUIRE MILES, ASL POET AND PERFORMING ARTIST EXTRAORDINAIRE

Some of the greatest artistic achievements in ASL poetry came not from a Deaf American, but a creative and talented Deaf woman from Wales named Dorothy Squire Miles. Welch writers have created many wonderful works of literatures, and Dot Miles carried on this great tradition in English and in American Sign Language.

Dorothy Squire Miles was born in North Wales in 1931, the youngest of five children. At the age of eight, she was stricken with cerebrospinal meningitis, which completely destroyed her hearing. We can only imagine what a painful loss this could be. But as they say, "When God shuts one door, He/She opens another." And so, Dot entered the Royal School for the Deaf in Manchester, England, and later the Mary Hare School in Berkshire, England. Here she discovered a new world of visual communication, a new visual language, British Sign Language—and new avenues for her creative and artistic talents. She was so successful in her school endeavors that, in 1957, she received a scholarship from the British Deaf Association to travel to the United States and enroll at Gallaudet University. There, she continued her creative and artistic achievements. She edited various literary magazines, winning prizes for both her prose writing and her poetry as well as for her acting. Some of her work was published in "The Silent Muse," an anthology of literary works published by the Gallaudet College Alumni Association.

One example of Dot Miles' artistry that is still celebrated today is the "Bison Fight Song," a chant that has been seen in the past 58 years by virtually every Gallaudet student. In 1960, the Gallaudet Audiology and Speech Department announced a competition for students to compose an official "Bison Fight Song" that could be spoken, sung, or signed at various athletic events. Lo and behold, Dorothy Miles won the competition with a short but powerful poem. Thereafter, the Gallaudet community, led by George Johnston, proceeded to create an ASL version of the song, using the 1-2, 1-2-3 rhythm of a typical Deaf chant. There was just one problem. Dot Miles song was too short for an extended ASL chant. So, the ASL chanters added lines from a poem by Robert Panara titled "The Bison Spirit" to create the extended ASL version of the Bison Song.

For more than half a century the "Bison Fight Song" has been performed at every homecoming and other major sports event. It has evolved through various incarnations to its present-day version. But it all started with Dorothy Miles. You can learn more about the "Bison Fight Song" through a history narrated by Hazel Pauline Bienvenue-Wood at https://www.youtube.com/watch?v=psfetUCGu0Y.

In 1961, Dorothy Miles received her BA with distinction from Gallaudet and began her career as a teacher and counselor for Deaf adults. However, her thirst for creative activities in ASL continued unabated and, in 1967, when the National Theatre of the Deaf was founded, she leaped at the chance and joined the company as an actress.

The National Theater of the Deaf was the first professional theater company that featured Deaf performers in sign language and voice productions. It had the distinction of performing on every continent, including Antarctica (where they performed for the crew of a Russian research ship docked there). In 1978, the company received a Tony Award for Theatrical Excellence. Clearly the National Theater of the Deaf was a resounding success with hearing audiences.

Not so with Deaf audiences. NTD's mantra, "You see and hear every word," meant that NTD coordinated its signing and voicing performances so well that hearing audiences would see a sign and, at the same time, hear the word for that sign. The Deaf performers had to produce signs in English word order and sign as fast as they could, since English and ASL have different rates of speed. Additionally, they used "artistic" signs to enhance the performance. As a result, Deaf audience members could understand almost nothing of the signed performances. To make things worse, some of the NTD performers blamed the Deaf audiences, saying they were not "sophisticated" enough to enjoy the performance, even though most of them had informal theater experiences at their clubs and organizations of the Deaf. The number of Deaf audience members dwindled to a mere handful of "sophisticated" Deaf people.

In 1971, NTD attempted to recapture its Deaf audiences by staging *My Third Eye*, an innovative work that explored the lives and culture of Deaf people. The work consisted of five episodes, and the second episode, "Sideshow" was co-directed by Joe Chaikin and Dorothy Miles, making her the first female Deaf professional theater director.

"Sideshow" presented the strange world of the hearing as seen by a ringmaster and a troupe of acrobats who lived in the world of the Deaf. They interacted with two hearing people contained in a cage like circus animals. The Deaf ringmaster demonstrated the effects on the hearing captives of some "puzzling" instruments, such as a whistle, a tape recorder, a party noise-maker and a telephone. The Deaf acrobats caricatured the cultural folkways of hearing people from the land of "blah-blah-blah," such as their obsession with the telephone, their fear of being touched and their constant desire to teach speech to Deaf people. In "putting the shoe on the other foot," the segment helped the hearing audience members become aware of how their beliefs and attitudes oppressed Deaf people.

The reaction from Deaf and hearing audiences to *My Third Eye* was quite divergent. Deaf audiences thought that *My Third Eye* was a smash hit and gave it many standing ovations. They loved it and called it the best play they had ever seen. They clapped long and loud because they identified with what was happening on state. In particular, they found that making fun of hearing people in "Sideshow," was hilarious fun.

Hearing audiences, on the other hand, gave My Third Eye mixed reviews. Accustomed to NTD's repertoire of classic works rendered in theatrical signs, they found the realistic and educational aspects of this new work difficult to adjust to. Most hearing critics wrote favorable reviews, but some felt that the work was more of "teaching exercise" than true theatre. Individual hearing audience members were more specific, "You have made me ashamed I am hearing," said one. Another said, "Where can I learn signs? I have two deaf children." Another complained, "Why are you so bitter? I just can't relate to you. Why do you want sympathy?"

Because of this mixed reaction, NTD never again presented a theater work about Deaf people and Deaf culture. Instead they resumed their tradition of transforming classical works into sign language and voice productions.

However, Dorothy Miles was just getting started. She later worked with a Deaf theater company, the Hartford Players, to write and direct *A Play of Our Own*, the first full-length play to present an authentic portrait of a Deaf family. The play was based on *Guess Who's Coming to Dinner*, a film about a white family whose attitudes were challenged when their daughter brought home a black man as her new fiancé, Dot Miles changed the story line to show a family of four Deaf people whose attitudes were challenged when the daughter brought home a hearing man as her fiancé, Unlike National Theater of the Deaf productions, **A Play of Our Own** did not provide voicing narrators so that audiences could watch every sign and not be distracted by spoken English. The performances were enthusiastically received by Deaf audiences as well as hearing fluent signers. It was performed in several locations in the U.S. and it inspired other playwrights such as Steven Baldwin to create sequels. It inspired Don Bangs to develop thirteen produced plays about the lives and struggles of Deaf people.

Even while she was involved in developing and performing in theater, Dorothy Miles continued to work on her poetry. Over the years, she and other Deaf poets had written many beautiful and inspiring poems in English that were then translated into sign language. But now she began to ask herself: how could she create poetry that could be expressed in a way that demonstrated the poetics of American Sign Language. If English poetry could produce rhymes, rhythms and other poetic elements, how could ASL also produce its own unique poetic elements.

In 1975, Dorothy Miles left the National Theater of the Deaf and relocated to California where she worked at California State University, Northridge and continued to explore the possibilities of ASL poetry. The following year, she published **Gestures: Poetry in Sign Language**" an illustrated book showing the range of her poetic creativity. Much of the book is a compilation of English-language poetry that Dorothy Miles created during her life time. Sprinkled among the selections are a number of new poems with rhythms and patterns that are based on American Sign Language. Dorothy Miles was the trailblazer for a new genre of ASL poetry.

Let's explore some of the ways that Dorothy Miles poetry incorporated the beauty and inspiration of ASL into wonderful poetic forms. First, we'll view her most famous poem, "Seasons." This is a Haiku poem, a traditional form of Japanese poetry. Haiku poems consist of 3 lines. The first and last lines of a Haiku have 5 syllables and the middle line has 7 syllables. Here are the words to Dot Miles haiku poem. Notice how they follow the 5-syllable, 7-syllable, 5-syllable form and present wonderful imagery.

SEASONS

(An Exercise in Haiku)

SPRING
Sunshine, borne on breeze
among singing trees, to dance
on rippled water.

SUMMER
Green depths and green heights,
clouds and quiet hours – slow, hot,
heavy on hands.

AUTUMN
Scattered leaves, a-whirl
in playful winds, turn to watch
people hurry by.

WINTER
Contrast: black and white;
bare trees, covered ground; hard ice,
soft snow; birth in death.

From *Gestures: Poetry in Sign Language* by Dorothy Miles. Copyright © 1976 by Joyce Media Inc. Reprinted by permission. joycemediainc.com

Now, let's see how this Haiku poem can be translated into an ASL poem that features many of the poetic elements of ASL Poetry.

MY ASL TUBE 5-20: SEASONS, AN ASL/ENGLISH POEM BY DOROTHY MILES

Dorothy Miles probably realized that a strict 5-7-5 Haiku format was not workable for an ASL version. Instead, she created new forms of poetic expression, using a variety of techniques. Here are examples of her techniques in creating ASL poetic forms by creating patterns based on sign parameters:

1. **HANDSHAPE:** In *Summer,* we can show the doldrums of the summer months by signing "slow, hot, heavy on hands" Notice that the signs are made by either "B" or "5" handshapes. In *Winter*, we can sign her words "bare trees" and "hard ice" with similar "clenched" handshapes.

   Can you find more examples of the handshape patterns in Dot Miles' poetry?

   _____

   _____

   _____

2. **MOVEMENT AND FLOW:** *Spring* opens with the line, "Sunshine, borne on breeze among singing trees," To sign these words, you would probably start with sunshine beaming from the right, being carried leftward by breezes, and causing the trees to "sing" on the left. The result is a beautiful series of movements from right to left.

   Can you find more examples of the movement patterns in Dot Miles' poetry?

   _____

   _____

   _____

3. **LOCATION:** *Autumn* presents the images of "Scattered leaves, a-whirl in playful winds, turn to watch people hurry by" which can be signed with just a "5" handshape representing the leaves. They are laid about on the ground, then swirling around and then coming to rest in a way that makes the "leaves" seem to be watching the people going by. With just a "5" handshape, all the changing locations enable the signer to tell a complete story.

Can you find more examples of the location patterns in Dot Miles' poetry?

_____

_____

_____

4. **ORIENTATION**: In *Summer*, the line, "slow, hot, heavy on hands" alternates between palm-out and palm-in. The in-and-out change of orientation as the hands descend from an upper to lower position is a fascinating pattern of poetic imagery.

Can you find more examples of the orientation patterns in Dot Miles' poetry?

_____

_____

_____

Dorothy Miles' poetry opened people's eyes to the creative possibilities for poetry based on ASL. Many other poets such as Clayton Valli and Ella Mae Lentz followed in her footsteps. However, there was a significant difference. Dorothy Miles tried to match the ASL signs and the English words in her poems so that an audience could "see and hear every word" which was the influence of National Theater of the Deaf. The later ASL poets dispensed with the need to match English and ASL versions and performed only in ASL with support from sign language interpreters. This made for a more natural rendition of ASL poetry. They even changed the sign for ASL poetry; during Dot Miles time, the sign for "poetry" was derived from the sign for "song," using a "p" handshape instead. The newer and more widely used sign mimics pulling the poem from the heart and offering it to the audience.

In 1977, Dorothy Miles returned to England and, for the next sixteen years, developed many creative projects promoting British Sign Language (BSL) and the British Deaf community. She helped establish the National Union of the Deaf's pioneering BBC series, "Open Door" which later led to the "See Hear" television series, still in operation to this day. She also worked with the British Deaf Association to promote the learning of BSL and developed the first teaching manual for BSL instructors. She was instrumental in setting up the Council for the Advancement of Communication with Deaf People and also helped compile a dictionary of BSL. Dorothy Miles worked on many other projects to promote BSL including the first university course for training Deaf people to become BSL instructors and the BBC book and video "BSL: A Beginner's Guide."

On January 30, 1993, Dorothy Miles died after falling from the window of her second-floor apartment. An inquest ruled that she took her own life as a result of severe depression.

Dorothy Miles was a significant figure in the development of innovative literary works in sign language on both sides of the Atlantic. Regarded as the "mother of sign language poetry," she passionately promoted Deaf culture in theater and poetry. In her honor, The Dorothy Miles Cultural Centre was established in England by a group of both Deaf and hearing friends. You can enjoy a biography of her life and work narrated in ASL:

MY ASL TUBE 5-21: DOROTHY MILES, ACTRESS AND POET EXTRAORDINAIRE

HOW DID I DO?

I hope you enjoyed all the things you learned in this chapter. You can use your new skills and knowledge to interact comfortably with Deaf people about their biological and social families. It's a good idea to check your progress. Below are the goals for the chapter along with a continuum from "I did great!" to "I need to work on this more." Write an "x" in the place that you feel reflects your progress in this chapter.

1. Describe the process involved in choosing a career and applying for and starting a new job.

   ←——————————————————————————————→

   I need to work on this more   I did great!

2. Modify signs to indicate daily, weekly, monthly, and annual routines as well as routines with more general time lines.

   ←——————————————————————————————→

   I need to work on this more   I did great!

3. Discuss personal qualities that you find among people at work.

   ←——————————————————————————————→

   I need to work on this more   I did great!

4. Describe some of the employment positions that Deaf people encounter in the world of work.

   ←——————————————————————————————→

   I need to work on this more   I did great!

5. Use some common finger-spelled abbreviations in the working world to communicate with Deaf employees.

   ←——————————————————————————————→

   I need to work on this more   I did great!

6. Summarize some typical mini-biographies of Deaf people in the world of work and compare them to their own autobiographies.

   ←——————————————————————————————→

   I need to work on this more   I did great!

7. Use non-manual markers (NMMs) to create conditional sentences that are used in the world of work or in other situations.

   ←——————————————————————————————→

   I need to work on this more   I did great!

8. Demonstrate how to ask for help or favors using intimate/casual, formal, and pleading approaches.

◄——►

I need to work on this more   I did great!

9. Describe some categories of activities that Deaf people are prone to engage in during retirement.

◄——►

I need to work on this more   I did great!

10. Outline some of the ways that Deaf people deal with dying or death as part of life in a Deaf world.

◄——►

I need to work on this more   I did great!

11. Describe how Deaf people can create ASL literature and folklore as exemplified by ABC and number stories.

◄——►

I need to work on this more   I did great!

12. Describe the life and achievements of the Deaf Actress and ASL poetess, Dorothy Squire Miles.

◄——►

I need to work on this more   I did great!

Becoming an Ally to the Deaf World

CHAPTER 6

INTRODUCTION

Congratulations! You've made a lot of progress in developing your ASL skills, increasing your knowledge of Deaf culture, and building a sensitivity and awareness when interacting with Deaf people. I am sure you can interact comfortably and develop many connections and associations with Deaf people. You can play a variety of roles: friend, co-worker, relative, bowling partner, student, teacher, Deaf coffee-night regular, and many other roles. As you interact with a variety of Deaf people, you will become more fluent in your ASL skills and more adept in your Deaf cultural knowledge.

Among the many roles you can play with members of the Deaf world, I would like for you to consider one important role: becoming an ally of Deaf people. What exactly is hearing ally? Why are they needed? What kind of actions does a hearing ally become involved in? After you finish this chapter, you will be able to:

1. **Describe the roles, goals, and actions of hearing allies of Deaf people.**

2. **Provide examples of power imbalance through a #hearingprivilege format.**

3. **Describe the concept of Deaf-Hearing power imbalances.**

4. **Demonstrate what hearing allies can do to correct hearing privilege and power imbalances.**

THE ASL CLUB

THE ROLE OF A HEARING ALLY IN THE DEAF WORLD

First of all, a hearing ally is a person who works with Deaf people to resist oppression and discrimination. Hearing allies strive to change attitudes of hearing people toward Deaf people. Their goal is to transform these attitudes from an audistic point of view, an attitude that hearing people are superior to Deaf people, to a positive perspective about Deaf people and Deaf culture. They do this in consultation with Deaf people about how best to support them as an ally.

Deaf people are a proud people and strongly advocate self-determination. You might have heard the famous statement about Deaf people made by Dr. I. King Jordan, the first Deaf president of Gallaudet University: "Deaf people can do anything that hearing people can do, except hear." A popular magazine, "Deaf Life," features many stories about Deaf people who have succeeded as doctors, EMTs, fire fighters, movie stars,

UFC champions, and many other fields. Based on these stories, we might be led to assume that Deaf people can do anything and that hearing allies are sort of superfluous.

Not so fast! Even though Deaf people believe they can do anything, they are confronted with a huge power imbalance when they interact with hearing people. A hearing ally could support Deaf people's efforts to reduce this power imbalance.

#HEARINGPRIVILEGE

A few years ago, some Deaf Facebookers started a hashtag called "Hearing Privilege" which was similar in to another popular hashtag, #whiteprivilege. Over a period of a few weeks, Deaf Facebookers contributed more than 200 examples demonstrating that hearing people could do anything they wanted compared Deaf people who were shackled by hearing society's limitations. I cannot list all the hashtag postings, but I will show you paraphrases of the more common posts. You can view the complete list by typing #hearingprivilege in the Face Book search page. Here are some paraphrases:

FAMILY RELATIONSHIPS

#hearingprivilege is being able to enjoy family gatherings and laugh at family jokes without any communication barriers, even though nobody knows any sign language.

EDUCATION

#hearingprivilege is being a child in a school for hearing children who is easily able to interact with the his or her fellow students and teachers without needing an interpreter. While a Deaf child is limited to communication via interpreters, many of whom are not fluent in ASL. OR, as hearing parents, they can easily participate in their children's school events such as parent-teacher conferences, PTA meetings, talent shows, football and basketball games and many other events without being left out. Deaf parents are often left out due to lack of interpreters.

MASS MEDIA

#hearingprivilege means clicking on a Face Book or You Tube video and understanding everything even though the majority of these videos are not captioned or being able to turn on the car radio in the morning and listen to news and information.

EMPLOYMENT

#hearingprivilege means being able to find a good and satisfying job, even though you live in a small town or being able to chat informally with your supervisor and convince him/her to give you a promotion. This is a different situation compared to Deaf people who are often denied a sign language interpreter, especially for informal chats.

PUBLIC SAFETY

#HearingPrivilege is being able to hear requests and commands from the police and not have them become upset and shout at you or shoot you because you cannot understand them.

HOSPITALS AND CLINICS

#hearingprivilege means being able to schedule a medical appointment in a timely manner, without needing to wait for several days or weeks for the medical office to find an interpreter. Or being able to easily communicate with your doctor or nurse, while Deaf patients may often be provided with an interpreter who cannot clearly communicate medical information.

EATING OUT

#HearingPrivilege is being able to communicate in your car to the drive-through order station at a fast-food restaurant and not being yelled at by the service people who don't understand why you didn't make a spoken order before you drove up to their window. Or sitting in a classy restaurant and NOT being offered a braille menu.

TRAVEL

#hearingprivilege means being at the airport and NOT being offered a wheelchair like when some Deaf people tell the agent they are Deaf. OR being able to understand all the valuable information from airport announcements about delays, changes of gates, flight cancellations, etc. without being left out in the cold.

There are many, many more pages of examples, most of them backed up by actual experiences. I would like to challenge you to view more examples presented in My ASL Tube and to write down the examples in the blanks below:

1. #hearingprivilege_____

_____

2. #hearingprivilege_____

_____

3. #hearingprivilege_____

_____

4. #hearingprivilege_____

_____

5. #hearingprivilege_____

_____

6. #hearingprivilege_____

_____

7. #hearingprivilege_____

_____

8. #hearingprivilege_____

_____

9. #hearingprivilege_____

_____

10. #hearingprivilege_____

_____

MY ASL TUBE 6-1: EXAMPLES OF #HEARINGPRIVILEGE

I hope you have gained an understanding of the constant struggles that Deaf people go through on a day-to-day basis. Hearing people don't have to deal with these struggles because the system works for them.

You may have noticed that the people in the video use different signs for "privilege." That is because this is a new concept and different Deaf people have different signs for this new concept. Below are some signs that are used to express "Hearing Privilege." I have added a rough description of the actual meaning of the sign. Also, the video shows various signs for "power relationships":

"Do what I want!"

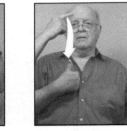
"my decision"

"permission/ privilege"

hearing

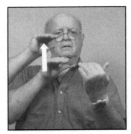
"higher status"

"I can easily do it"

"I'll go ahead and do it"

DEAF-HEARING POWER IMBALANCES

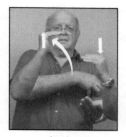

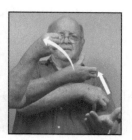

Power equality   power imbalance   empowerment   disempowerment

Another way to understand the struggles of Deaf people during their interactions with hearing people is to examine the power dynamics between Deaf and hearing people. For example, if a school for Deaf children refuses to allow the children to use sign language to communicate but instead forces them to use only speech and lipreading, there is clearly a power imbalance between the hearing adult school staff and the Deaf children. The hearing staff holds virtually all the power over the Deaf children's mode of communication, while the children have virtually no power and can only communicate in signs when they are by themselves and not under the control of the teachers or staff.

Perhaps you have heard about a new fad in the child development field that encourages parents of hearing babies to communicate by signing with them. Hearing infants and toddlers can express themselves with signs much earlier than they can communicate through speech. So, many, many parents of hearing babies buy books and attend workshops that show them how to "sign with your baby." While the Deaf community is proud that their language can make life better for those hearing babies, they are also angry about the double standard employed here. Why is it okay for parents of hearing babies to use sign language while so-called oralist professionals discourage parents of Deaf babies from communicating with signs. Clearly there is a huge power imbalance here.

There is plenty of evidence from American and international researchers that using sign language with Deaf babies and toddlers facilitates their development of ASL and English language skills. So, to refuse to allow sign language in the education of Deaf babies and toddlers is considered "language deprivation" by members of the Deaf community. Deaf leaders and parents of Deaf children are challenging the speech only power imbalance by advocating for laws that support a bilingual ASL-English approach for the education of Deaf children. They have formed a national organization called LEAD-K (Language Equality and Acquisition for Deaf Kids) with the goal of helping Deaf children from birth to five years of age to acquire the language they need to be kindergarten-ready. Many of their state chapters have lobbied their state legislatures for laws that support this goal. Unfortunately, oralist organizations such as the Alexander Graham Bell Association of the Deaf have tried to maintain the power imbalance by interfering with the LEAD-K lobbying. Despite this, so far, five state governments have adopted the LEAD-K's position, an outcome that bodes well for the education of Deaf children in these states.

This is just one of the many power imbalances that exist between Deaf and hearing people. Trudy Suggs, the Deaf owner of TS Writing Service, has written a masterful and comprehensive description of how Deaf people are often disempowered by hearing people. She points out that, even though the Deaf community has made a lot of progress in fields such as education, communication access, discrimination issues, etc., the cumulative effect of many everyday disempowering events and situations contribute to a major sense of disempowerment among Deaf individuals. You can read about this at:

http://www.trudysuggs.com/a-quick-look-at-everyday-disempowerment-of-deaf-people

WHAT ROLES SHOULD A HEARING ALLY PLAY?

As you have learned in previous chapters, another word for a continuing support for "hearing privilege" is the word "audism." This belief system promotes the idea that people who hear are superior in their attitudes and abilities than are Deaf people. Audism often creates power imbalances whether or not hearing people are aware of it. So, your role as a hearing ally of the Deaf community is to combat audism in all of its forms. Here are some actions you can take to support Deaf people's efforts to take back the personal powers they have been denied for so long:

1. HELP EXTINGUISH AUDIST ATTITUDES AND BELIEFS

As an ASL communicator and a friend of Deaf people, you will almost certainly be asked friends and acquaintances about why you have been learning ASL. When these people express audist attitudes and beliefs, you need to provide them with correct information about ASL and Deaf culture. When doing so, it's best to be honest, be gentle, and be loving. Obviously, you won't want a negative or demeaning comment slide so share your honest point of view. Don't get into an argument because almost all arguments end with the opposing sides even more strongly attached to their points of view. Avoid criticizing the audist friend but instead, be gentle and share your own beliefs and attitudes. Finally, be loving and do what you can to help this person to mature and grow out of his/her audist beliefs.

Outside of your circle of friends and family members, you probably will need to take much stronger actions. You may encounter newspaper articles, television programs, public statements by politicians, and many other media expressions that disempower Deaf people. In this case, you need to respond strongly in opposition to the disempowerment of the Deaf community by challenging the actions of the media.

Another situation that needs your action is when you are with Deaf friends and people who are supposed to be serving your friends will try to disempower them by ignoring them or treading them rudely. First, ask your Deaf friends if they want you to intervene and, if the answer is yes, either interpret for them or speak out to the rudeskies.

2. SEEK TO REALLY UNDERSTAND DEAF PEOPLE'S POINTS OF VIEW

You can't really be an ally if you don't know and understand what Deaf people are thinking. Perhaps you are a little nervous about prying into their experience and beliefs. Don't worry; Once you gain their trust, they'll be happy to share their thoughts and feelings with you. You can make a good start by using the magic signed phrase "I'm curious" and take it from there. Some hearing allies may want to give advice or suggest solutions. I recommend that you just listen and don't suggest anything. If you can't stand not making a suggestion, just ask your Deaf friends what they plan to do. Then, if they ask for it, you can give your opinion. By paying attention and listening, you'll grow in your understanding and support of Deaf people. In addition, you'll increase your own self-awareness.

3. CONFRONT YOUR OWN AUDISM

You may think you're a good person and would never do anything that supports and promotes audism. Think again. There are many actions you might take without being aware that your actions are audistic. For example, do you try to communicate with your Deaf friends without checking to make sure they can see you clearly? When you are chatting with Deaf friends and a hearing non-signing friend starts talking to you, do you cut away from your Deaf friends and speak to your hearing friend without signing? Do you assume that a Deaf friend who applies for a job in your company shouldn't be hired because of his/her disability? Do you post videos on Facebook without captions? These are all examples of a hearing people not taking into consideration the needs of their Deaf friends. Go deep. Explore how you handle situations by asking whether or not it causes harm to Deaf people.

4. USE YOUR HEARING PRIVILEGE TO SUPPORT DEAF MOVEMENTS

Are you a member of the NAD? Your state Deaf association? Do you attend Deaf rallies at your city, state, or federal capitol? Do you send letters and emails and make phone calls to government agencies and businesses to make sure they consider the needs of Deaf people? These and other actions can help Deaf people succeed in getting people in positions of power to listen to and address the concerns of the Deaf community. It is an unfortunate fact of life that these leaders will be more likely to listen to a hearing person. Even so, if you express your support for Deaf community causes, and encourage them to make connections with the Deaf community, they will be more inclined to do so. We hope.

On the other hand, Deaf movements belong to Deaf people, so don't attempt to become a leader or take over the movement. Many, many times, at Deaf movement events such as rallies, testimonies, conferences, protests, etc., the media will almost always try to interview hearing people about Deaf people. Either they may have no idea how to connect with Deaf leaders or they will consider their point of view not worth the printer's ink or video footage for their programs. When approached for an interview by a journalist or a media figure, firmly direct them to the leaders of the Deaf movement. Try to find an interpreter to facilitate the interview or, if none is available, do your best to support the Deaf leader's efforts to be heard.

You can also volunteer for these Deaf movements or donate to the many Gofundme campaigns that support them. Or, if you donate funds to a program that targets the general population, you can request that your donation be used to support Deaf people's concerns and interests.

5. BE INCLUSIVE WITH DEAF PEOPLE IN YOUR AFFAIRS

As we learned in Chapter 3, Deaf people have two families, their biological families and their Deaf and signing social families. You can make an effort to include Deaf people in both families. Invite them to attend your family affairs and hire an interpreter to make them feel a part of the festivities. Communication access at picnics, weddings, graduation parties, and even funerals will provide Deaf and hearing people with opportunities to learn about and understand each other's worlds.

Of course, many Deaf people will decline your invitation because of past negative experiences at such events. Be creative and find ways to include Deaf people in the events. A year ago, a good friend of mine who ran a Deaf program within her college's English Department unexpectedly died. A few months later, the family arranged for a memorial service to honor this professor. A sizeable group of Deaf people attended. Guess how many Deaf people were invited to share their memories of their wonderful relations with the professor. Zero! Only hearing people shared their memories. Every speaker mentioned the Deaf program in passing but it was as if we were not there. Imagine what a different and more wonderful experience the memorial service would have been if a Deaf person had shared their memories of their wonderful hearing friend. Both Deaf and hearing people would grow in awareness and understanding from this kind of experience.

In conclusion, I hope this chapter has given you many insights about how to be an effective ally for Deaf people. As you become more aware of hearing privilege and power imbalances, you can help support and model activities that seek to correct these imbalances. This way, you can bring Deaf and hearing people together in a world that respects and supports both communities.

HOW DID I DO?

I hope you enjoyed all the things you learned in this chapter. You can use your new skills and knowledge to interact comfortably with Deaf people and be an ally if you so choose. It's a good idea to check your progress. Below are the goals for the chapter along with a continuum from "I did great!" to "I need to work on this more." Draw an "x" in the place that you feel reflects your progress in incorporating the Student Learning Objectives into your repertoire of choices.

1. Describe the roles, goals, and actions of hearing allies of Deaf people.

   I need to work on this more   I did great!

2. Provide examples of power imbalances caused by hearing privilege.

   I need to work on this more   I did great!

3. Describe the concept of Deaf-Hearing power imbalances.

   I need to work on this more   I did great!

4. Demonstrate what hearing allies can do to correct hearing privilege and power imbalances.

   I need to work on this more   I did great!